MADRAS 1922 HAND BOOK

# INDIAN SCIENCE CONGRESS

MADRAS 1922 HAND BOOK

# INDIAN SCIENCE CONGRESS

FOR THE USE OF MEMBERS ATTENDING THE NINETH MEETING TO BE HELD AT MADRAS FROM THE THIRTIETH OF JANUARY TO THE FOURTH OF FEBRUARY, 1922

GYAN

*Published by*

Gyan Publishing House
5, Ansari Road
Daryaganj, New Delhi-110002
Phone: 011-47034999, 9811692060
E-mail: books@gyanbooks.com

*Distribution Network*
gyanbooks.com
India, USA, Canada, UK, Australia, France



ISBN : 978-81-212-3619-5 (PB)
First Published, Madras, 1921

2nd Impression 2020

*Printed at:* Gyan Press, Delhi.



**Madras 1922 Hand Book**
**Indian Science Congress**

# FOREWORD

An Indian Science Congress was first suggested in 1914 by Dr. Simonsen, of Madras, and Mr. P. C. MacMahon, of Lucknow, and the scheme took practical shape under the auspices of a Committee of the Asiatic Society of Bengal, who arranged the first meeting, which was held in Calcutta in that year. Sir S. G. Burrard, F. R. S., Surveyor-General, and Sir A. H. Hayden, F.R.S., Director of the Geological Survey, were chiefly instrumental in securing recognition of the Congress by Government and by the Council of the Asiatic Society of Bengal without which the new Association would probably not have flourished. As it is, successful meetings have been held in Calcutta, Madras, Lucknow, Bangalore, Lahore, Bombay, Nagpur, and again in Calcutta, each winter since 1914. Notwithstanding the war, the institution has survived, has grown steadily in influence and appears now to have a healthy hold on life. Like the British Association for the Advancement of Science on which in its small beginnings the Congress has been modelled, its aims are threefold :—(*i*) to furnish opportunities for scientific workers to get in touch with men working on allied subjects ; (*ii*) to encourage research ; (*iii*) to make scientific knowledge accessible to the general public.

This handbook has been prepared for the ninth meeting of the Indian Science Congress, to provide members with such information as to the City and Presidency of Madras, and the scientific work that is being carried on there, as will be of interest to them, especially to those who are visiting Madras for the first time, or who are but little acquainted with this part of India.

No complete guide to Madras has been attempted, but merely a collection of articles on subjects which it is thought members would like information about. Each article, however, is written by some one specially qualified to write it, and in this way the book will be perhaps of greater value than a more systematic compilation in which much of the information must of necessity be given second hand. The editor also imagines that visitors to the Congress will have no time to read long accounts of the Presidency and its activities, but will wish for some information on such points, as short as possible, and at the same time accurate. It is believed that both these desiderata have been secured.

The authors of the various articles are for the most part very busy men, and the editor feels, and hopes that members of the Congress will also feel, a real gratitude to them for giving up time they can ill spare to the writing of this handbook.

CLIVE NEWCOMB.

## Past Presidents

1914. The Hon'ble Justice Sir Ashutosh Mukerjee, *Kt.*, C.S.I., M.A., D.L., F.A.S.B.

1915. Major-General W. B. Bannerman, C.S.I., M.D., D.Sc., I.M.S.

1916. Colonel Sir Sidney Burrard, K.C.S.I., F.A.S.B., F.R.S., R.E.

1917. Sir Alfred Gibbs Bourne, K.C.I.E., D.Sc., F.R.S.

1918. Dr. Gilbert T. Walker, C.S.I., M.A., F.R.S.

1919. Lt.-Colonel Sir Leonard Rogers, *Kt.*, C.I.E., M.D., B.S., F.R.C.P., F.R.C.S., F.R.S., F.A.S.B., I.M.S.

1920. Sir Prafulla Chandra Ray, *Kt.*, C.I.E., Ph.D., D.Sc., F.A.S.B.

1921. The Hon'ble Sir Rajendra Nath Mookerjee, K.C.I.E.

# CONTENTS

# THE HISTORY OF MADRAS

## I

FORT SAINT GEORGE was founded in 1639. Some years earlier the English had built themselves a small fort at Armagon, a little to the northward; but they had been unable to procure cloth or escape attack there, and a mere factory-house in the small and crowded town of Masulipatam, then their head-quarters, proved too insecure and uncertain. The English factors accordingly looked for a site offering some natural protection against attack, such as the Dutch already possessed at Pulicat. They found what promised to serve their need in a sandy spit of land protected on the west and south by a river which they called the Triplicane River and we the Cooum. There they built a castle, much like one of those square castles which still survive at Home in picturesque ruin, with bastions at each corner. This they named Fort Saint George.

Its eastern face ran parallel with and somewhat to the east of the Secretariat. It contained lodgings for the Company's servants, quarters for the Governor, a great hall in which all dined and where prayers were read morning and evening, warehouses and guard-rooms.

Round this as a centre sprang up a small town, where Portuguese from San Thomé, Armenians, Jews, and other strangers, with a few English, were allowed to build houses, at first of one storey only so as not to command the fort. This was called the White Town, in contra-distinction to the Indian town which grew up further to the north called Black Town. In a short while the garden walls of the houses in the White Town came to form a continuous enclosure bordering the river on the south and west. Presently the sea-front and the space between the sea and the river to the north were also walled in. Bastions, or points, as our ancestors called them, were added. Thus a larger fortified enclosure came into existence, which, though for long still called the White Town, was at last dignified with the name of the original fort, now shrunk to a mere citadel. Two churches were built in this enclosure — one, the Roman Catholic

Church of Saint Andrew near the northern wall; the other, Saint Mary's, built in 1680 and still standing just south of the citadel. Gradually the importance of the citadel declined; citizens were permitted to build a second storey on their houses; the real defences became the walls and bastions of the White Town, and the original fort was converted early in the eighteenth century into quarters for the Company's servants.

In the centre of this original fort had stood what was called the fort-house. In 1694 this was pulled down and a new building erected. This now forms the centre portion of the Secretariat.

Near to it stands another vestige of this old Madras. What is now the office of the Accountant-General was originally the residence of an Armenian merchant, Nazar Jacob Jan. From his successor Shawmier Sultan the house was acquired for the Company. Clive once lived in it. There he was lodged when for a few days he visited Madras in 1765. There for fifty years the Governor gave his concerts, his entertainments, his dances, his dinners which commenced at three, and after an interval for repose, were renewed in the form of supper.

## II

Such were the beginnings, such the vestiges which remain, of the original Fort Saint George, to the north lay, as I have said, the Black Town. Such was the security felt beneath the guns of the fort that the latter contained probably over 100,000 Indians by 1700. This assemblage of men under an alien rule is an eloquent testimony to the troubles of the land. Soon after Madras was founded, Sivaji's father, Shahji, came sweeping south on behalf of his master, the Adil Shah, King of Bijapur. As that power waned, the Kutub Shah, Kings of Golconda, secured the upper hand in the Carnatic, and less than twenty years later Aurangzib and his generals not only overthrew the Kutub Shah dynasty at Golconda, but established the Moghul power much further south. Arcot became the capital of a Moghul subah; Gingee became a Moghul fortress.

This, in fact, made little difference to Madras. Except for a brief period early in the first decade of the eighteenth century, when Aurangzib was definitely hostile and his Subahdar Da'ud Khan blockaded the English settlement, the time passed quietly, without any astonishing events. Not until more than a century after its foundation was Fort Saint George seriously imperilled.

This was fortunate, because its means of defence were not great. As a fortress it was contemptible. 'Were I the Governor,' said an English Naval Captain who knew it well, 'I should never sleep sound at night when the French had five hundred men to spare at Pondicherry.' In this respect Madras resembled almost every other fortress that Europeans held in the tropics at that time. They were all ill-built, ill-repaired, ill-provisioned, ill-garrisoned. This was but natural in a climate where timber rots and gun-powder decays with great rapidity unless protected with unusual care, and the garrison about matched the walls to be defended. The recruits were of the poorest quality. Who that could earn any sort of living in England would join the Company's service and get knocked on the head, or seized by a flux for 10*d*. a day? Nor were the officers such as to convert this bad material into efficient soldiers. Few had ever seen active service, those who had were old and worn out; those who had not were ignorant and careless of their duty. Neither the Company nor its Council at Madras troubled much about these things. They were content so long as they could keep the Nawab of Arcot in a good temper, and secure a large quantity of the coast calicoes, muslins and chintzes for the Company's investment.

## III

The penalty for this carelessness was paid when war broke out with France in 1744. At first the safety of Madras seemed sufficiently well secured by the English Squadron that came under Commodore Barnett. But Barnett died of a fever; and the command descended to Captain Peyton, the least enterprising Naval Commander of an unenterprising age. He retired hurriedly from the coast in 1740, after a very give-and-take engagement with a French Squadron which had been fitted out at Mauritius under La Bourdannais. The French Commander at once besieged Madras, which capitulated with celerity. The French bombardment had killed only six persons.

For the next three years Madras remained in the hands of the French; but it was restored in 1749 under the Treaty of Aix-la-Chapelle. Meanwhile the Council of Fort Saint David, immediately north of

Cuddalore, had conducted English affairs, and until early in 1752 that settlement continued to be the head-quarters of the Presidency. In 1752, however, the Government was once more transferred to Madras.

Meanwhile there had broken out that private war between the two Companies, French and English, which led to a large number of new things. The two Companies were supporting rival princes, therefore the English were no longer able to keep themselves from the complications of internal politics. Again the war was not only private, but also a war on land; the Company could no longer rely on the navy, but had to increase its land forces. Thus, on the one hand, the miserable and ill-trained garrison of perhaps 200 men expanded into a body of between one and two thousand, exercised in arms, hard-bitten, hard-trained, hard-disciplined men, as tough fighters as could be found anywhere in the world. They were supplemented by a large and growing body of sepoys, whom the French were the first to use, but whom the English were the first to train and discipline.

The private war between the Companies lasted some five years (1749—1754). The details of the struggle cannot here be related. No fighting took place in the immediate neighbourhood of Madras. Then came a short truce, which lasted till the outbreak of the Seven Years' War. The news of this reached Madras at the end of 1756. Meanwhile Siraj-ud-daulah had attacked Calcutta, and Clive had been despatched to relieve the position of the English in Bengal. The result was the overthrow of Siraj-ud-daulah, and the establishment of a virtual supremacy of the English by the men who had been trained to war against the French in the Carnatic.

The Seven Years' War was contested in South India with great stubbornness. The forces of the French and English Companies were supplemented by the forces of the respective Crowns. For the first two years the French had a great superiority of force; and after over-running almost all the surrounding country, the French Commander, Lally, laid siege to Madras at the end of 1758.

Fort Saint George was then a fortress very different from that which had capitulated to the French attack in three days in 1746. Soon after the Presidency had been re-established here in 1752, the reform of the fortifications had been set about. In place of the old irregular quadrilateral, with feeble curtains and irregular bastions, was planned a new and larger fortress of the most approved type, to make room for which the river was diverted from its former channel.

The new fort was in general plan much like a half moon, with its straight side towards the sea. To the landward were traced out a complicated series of works, with ditch, and counter-scarp, and ravelins, sheltering the ramparts themselves, and all alike hidden from the enemy's view by the lofty crest of the great glacis which sloped smoothly away from the fortifications themselves. These works were all of a most temporary nature. Almost all were earthworks faced with turf, but they were skilfully devised and heavily armed.

All through December, 1758, and January, 1759, Lally's batteries swept the northern face of Fort Saint George from entrenchments that ran (roughly) in a semi-circle from the Law Courts to the General Hospital. At one point they did much damage. The enemy pushed forward up the slope of the glacis in zig-zag saps until they reached the crest, but there they endeavoured in vain to open a battery. A similar fate attended their efforts to open the works by mining. At last, having exhausted themselves in the attempt, they withdrew sullenly and reluctantly. They had meant to burn the Black Town which had given them shelter during the siege, but the arrival of English reinforcements compelled them to withdraw without doing so.

This triumphant resistance marked the turning-point of the war in South India. The tide of battle rolled southward, towards Pondicherry. Coote overthrew Lally in pitched battle at Wandiwash. Soon after he was able to lay siege to Pondicherry. In January, 1761, it capitulated, and before the year was out, the great rival of Madras had been reduced to a shapeless heap of ruins. Its fortifications, its public buildings, the great palace from which Dupleix had hoped to rule all the country from the Kistna to Cape Comorin were utterly demolished, so that there was not left one stone standing on another. This was the fate Lally had designed for Madras.

## IV

From that day forward Madras was the capital of the Carnatic. Twenty years of vigorous rivalry had ended in the final overthrow of the French

Power. Only once more were the French to intervene actively in South Indian politics, and then not by the power of their settlement, but by an expedition despatched from Europe. Madras was not yet the capital of South India. About the same time that the English had definitely beaten the French, the great soldier of fortune, Haider 'Ali, had established his power in Mysore. In the last forty years of the eighteenth century there were two wars with Hyder 'Ali and two more with his son, Tipu Sultan. The first two were unfortunate for the English. They were not strong enough to counter the rapid and varied blows which Hyder 'Ali was able to deliver with the help of his cavalry. First General Joseph Smith, and later Sir Eyre Coote spent all their efforts on endeavouring on foot to chase mounted men out of the Carnatic. Naturally they could not succeed. In the two later wars Cornwallis and Wellesley pushed the English forces boldly into the enemy's country. Bangalore was twice taken; Seringapatam was threatened once and taken once. Its capture in 1799 left Madras without a rival in material power. Between 1760 and 1799 Fort Saint George had become not the head-quarters of a battalion, or of a brigade, as we reckon strength now-a-days, but of an army, including four regiments of Europeans, and twenty or more battalions of sepoys, a brigade of artillery, and a couple of brigades of horse.

The result of this extension of material force corresponded with the political growth of the Presidency. Down to 1793 the only regions directly governed by the English were the Northern Circars, as the four most northern districts of the Presidency were then called, and the modern district of Chingleput, then called the Company's jagir. In 1793 an arrangement was made with the Nawab of Arcot to place the principal *poligars* of Tinnevelly and Arcot under English control. The third Mysore War had added Salem to the English dominions. The fourth Mysore War had added the Ceded Districts — Bellary, Cuddapah, and Anantapur. Lastly, in 1801, after much political trouble with the Nawab, the whole of his dominions were taken over, and he became a pensioner in the stately palace which he had built for himself at Chepauk, and which is now occupied by the Board of Revenue. Thus the Presidency was formed much as it stands to-day, save that the districts of South Kanara and Malabar were transferred to Madras from Bombay.

## V

Thus the Presidency came into being as the result of a series of events in the second half of the eighteenth century. The power which centred in Fort Saint George had expanded, just as the fortress itself had grown from garden-walls surrounding a castle into elaborate works of eighteenth century defence. In like manner the system of Government which for two hundred and fifty years has been directed from that spot of ground where the Secretariat still stands, had been developed. For the first century of its existence it was as simple as the walls which protected it. It was composed of some ten or twelve men who held the chief commercial offices — the accountant, the two warehouse-keepers, the paymaster, and so forth. Their great business, when they sat once every year, was to settle the contract with the merchants who were supplying the cloth for the Company's investment, and when they met to take each his share in examining the cloth that had been brought in. Next in importance were their meetings to discuss the suitable punishment for some disorder that had taken place, as when two factors had drawn their swords on each other, or when a warehouse in the

Black Town had been broken into. Their political functions, apart from the administration of the settlement, were limited to an occasional letter of compliment, and interchange of presents with some local potentate.

This lasted for about a century. From 1749 for fifty years the Company's government developed great political power, without acquiring a correspondent administrative responsibility. The political determination of the Company's, and in great part of the Nawab's, conduct lay with the Madras Government, but the administration of the country was the Nawab's. Even the Company's jagir which lay around Madras was for long farmed out to the Nawab as renter. Indeed, he could not bear the least appearance of foreign intervention.

The result was half-a-century of abominable Government, during which the Nawab fleeced the people in order to procure the means of bribing the Company's Government to support his policy, while the English looked on, vaguely reprobating the manner of administration, but regarding its evils as inherent in every Indian Government.

An improvement, however, set in when the Company, from about 1780, began to appoint

Governors from Home. The first of these was Lord Macartney; others in the late eighteenth century and the early nineteenth century were Lord Hobart, Lord Clive (son of the victor of Plassey), and Lord William Bentinck, who later on became Governor-General. These men fresh from England were less tolerant of the abuses they encountered, which struck them more forcibly because they had not grown used to them. Under the impulsion of these men and their successors, the modern system of administration was developed.

## VI

This was accompanied by a remarkable, though unchronicled, concentration of the military forces of the Presidency. Under the Nawabs the collection of the revenue had been a military operation. Every parganah had had its military establishment, because the payment of taxes could only be secured by a show of force. The English inherited the system. In the early years of the nineteenth century you find garrisons all over the country — at the head-quarters of every district, and in numberless forts besides. Fort Saint George remained the head-quarters of the Madras Army; but there were large cantonments at Saint Thomas' Mount, at Pallaveram, at Poonamallee, at Wallajabad, at Vellore; to the south at Trichinopoly, Tanjore and Tinnevelly; to the north at Bellary, at Ellore, at Masulipatam, at Aska. But as the habit of English rule strengthened and as the idea of a rule of law quite distinct from, and above, any ruler's mere whim gradually took root, this ostentation of military force became unnecessary. The garrisons were therefore reduced, withdrawn, amalgamated. Their purpose ceased to be a military occupation of the country, but its protection. Meanwhile Fort Saint George remained just as it had been built by Paul Benfield and others in the eighteenth century. Its calculated irregularities, its maze of defences, its drawbridges, its great gates, remain mute witnesses of all the changes that a century and a half have brought about. That lowering archway of Saint George's Gate saw Clive pass under it; saw Du Pré go out to accept Hyder's terms of peace at Saint Thomas' Mount; saw a terrified runner bring Sir Hector Munro's hurried note announcing that the same foe had destroyed a detachment of his army; saw the troops march out that were to capture Seringapatam and slay its master ; and as the years passed, it saw too that the marching men grew fewer and less frequent. If the fort has ceased to echo with the salutes of victories, it has also ceased to be the bridle, the sign of domination, of the city that surrounds it.

R.H.D.

## THE OLDEST BRITISH BUILDING IN INDIA—A BRIEF SKETCH

OF all the places of interest in Madras, Fort Saint George is, from a British point of view, the most interesting; and of all the buildings within the Fort none is so rich in historic remains and associations as the venerable Church of Saint Mary, which, though not the oldest European, is certainly the oldest British building in India.

The Church owes its origin to the energy and devotion of the indomitable Sir Streynsham Master, who inaugurated his appointment as Agent to the East India Company in 1678, by the building of a suitable place of worship within the walls of the Fort. It must be remembered, of course, that the original Fort was confined within a very small area, where now the Secretariat stands. Previously to Master's time, that is to say, for about thirty-eight years, religious services had been conducted in what, on other occasions, served as the dining-room of the Factory House. Divine service was held twice daily and a fine inflicted for absence. It throws a light on Master's independence of character — an independence which eventually cost him his post — that the Church was built solely by the efforts and subscriptions of the Governor and his officers, without any appeal to, or permission from, the Company's Directors in London. The amount subscribed, 805 pagodas, was deemed sufficient to commence the work, and the excavations were begun on March 25 (Lady Day), 1678, just outside the south curtain of the inner fort. Though there is no entry recording the fact, the architect is usually considered to have been Edward Foule, the Master Gunner, who appears to have executed certain structural work about this time, but it is believed by others that Foule was in England at the time, and that the work had been completed by William Dixon, Chief Gunner, before his arrival. The Church, a worthy monument of his public work, was completed the year before Master was dismissed by the Company, as 'thinking himself too good or too big' and possessing 'intolerable presumption and indiscretion'. The new Church was consecrated for Divine service and dedicated to the

Blessed Virgin Mary on the 28th day of October, 1680, by the then Chaplain, Rev. Richard Portman, by virtue of an 'instrument' enabling him to act for the Bishop of London, within whose diocese, strange to say, India then was! To quote from the Council minutes, 'The ceremony was performed in very good order and concluded with vollies of small shot fired by the whole garrison drawn out and the cannon round the fort.' The anniversary of the dedication is celebrated every year with fitting ceremonial down to the present time.

The internal dimensions of the building are of their original size, namely, 86 feet by 56 feet. The tower was not part of the original building, but stood apart from the Church. It was built by order of Sir John Goldsborough at the end of the seventeenth century, but was not connected up to the end of Church until much later. The spire was added at the beginning of the eighteenth century. Some old prints show the tower without the spire. With this exception the fabric of the Church remains practically as it was when first built. There are certain unusual characteristics about the actual building, in which it differs from others in the Fort; one of these is the exceptional thickness of the walls and of the roof, which latter is of the 'waggon' or rounded shape, making it bomb-proof. The reason for this lay in the fact that the builders intended their Church to be capable, not only of withstanding violent storms, but also impregnable to enemy assault. History has shewn justification for their hopes. The Church was at the time of its erection the only bomb-proof building in the Fort, and though one well-directed modern shell would, no doubt, level it to the ground, nevertheless during all these years it has stood more or less intact, and though profane use was in the original 'surrender' provided against, it was for the above reasons found imperative to utilize Saint Mary's as a barrack and granary during the second French siege of Madras, in the middle of the eighteenth century, and again afterwards during the attack of Hyder 'Ali.

Another noteworthy characteristic of the edifice is that, as far as possible, the builders avoided using wood on account of fires; with, of course, the exception of doors and windows.

The vestries at the east end of the Church were not part of the original building, but were added less than a hundred years ago, and slight alterations made in the shape of the east end of the nave. But the main building remains with these small exceptions precisely as when built by our forefathers, and stands as a testimony to their thoroughness and ability.

Originally there was no actual 'churchyard' surrounding the Church, but those who died within the Fort, whether merchants, soldiers, sailors or their relatives, were buried in what was originally called the 'Guava Garden,' and nearly four thousand interments took place there. Of late years the new Law Courts have been built on the site of this old cemetery. Long before this during the second French attack on Madras, the Chief Engineer, Mr. (afterwards Sir John) Call, petitioned the Council for permission to demolish all the large monuments and tombs. He appears to have been a highly efficient and distinguished officer, but with a strong predilection for demolition. At any rate he reported to the Select Committee that during the siege they had 'suffered great inconvenience from the tombs at the burying-ground . . . which not only protected the enemy from our shot but afforded them a cover equally safe against our shells' and hoping 'they would be pleased to give orders for removing this evil'. Whereupon both the tombs and the walls which enclosed them were removed. Two large monuments were, however, spared to mark the site of the old 'Guava Garden,' and these are the tombs of David Yale, son of Governor Elihu Yale, and of the Ponney family. The new burial-ground was located on the Island on the north-west side, and is now known as the Saint Mary's Cemetery. The flat tombstones were brought over and placed round the Church, probably in much the same position as they are now. But, afterwards, during the siege of Hyder 'Ali, they were again removed and utilized for various purposes, some, doubtless, as gun-platforms in the Fort judging by the deep notches cut into the edges. It was not until the beginning of the nineteenth century that they were re-collected and restored to their former position, namely, round the east, north and west sides of the Church. When the Capuchin Church of Saint Andrew was demolished after the Peace of Aix-la-Chapelle, many of the gravestones were removed and placed here with the others: these are marked *R.C.* and are, many of them, inscribed in Portuguese, as well as Latin and Tamil.

The slabs are of 'Charnockite,' the name given to the gneiss, out of which Job Charnock's tomb was made, and in spite of exposure to weather are in a good state of preservation. A former Governor of Madras, the Duke of Buckingham and Chandos, produced an album containing plates of all the stones. This book, in the Chaplain's charge, is of considerable interest and value, as only a very limited number of copies were printed. The inscriptions upon the slabs are as varied as they are interesting, commemorating as they do many well-known persons. That of Elizabeth Baker, the wife of Aaron Baker, the first President and Governor of the Fort, is the most ancient of these. It is not, perhaps, generally known that this is the oldest British inscription in India.

Many distinguished persons are buried within the Church, but neither the exact number of interments nor the precise location of certain of them is known. Four Governors lie in the graves at the east end, of whom the most famous is Sir Thomas Munro, *Bart.*, and the most interesting Lord Pigot; the former because of his public work, and the latter on account of his impeachment by members of his own Council. The fact that there is no inscription over his grave has been thought to signify that there were discreditable circumstances attached to his arrest, but an examination of the contemporary records proves that Lord Pigot was in high favour with the Company throughout his career, and orders for his reinstatement were quickly issued, but arrived after his death.

There are several very beautiful monuments inside the Church, notably those sculptured by Flaxman and Bacon, but nearly all are worthy of a careful inspection.

The gallery, at the west end of the Church, is of intricate and beautiful workmanship; it originally extended along both sides of the nave and was probably built for the purpose of accommodating musicians. After the second French siege it was considerably enlarged in order to allow of an organ being placed there. Previously to this it had been used as the Governor's seat. The Mayor had a 'handsome' seat allotted to him in the middle aisle, where he sat, with his maces each side of him, 'next below the clerk's desk'.

The Font is of that same substance of which it has been mentioned the outside grave-stones are made, the black Charnockite brought from

Pallaveram. Its interest lies not only in the fact that it is probably the oldest object in the Church, but that the three daughters of Job Charnock were baptized therein. This fact is recorded in the Baptismal registers. The well-known story of Job Charnock's rescue, and eventual marriage to the beautiful Hindu widow, whom he rescued from 'Sati,' is borne out by an inscription in Saint John's, Calcutta, a copy of which has, by the kindness of Her Excellency Lady Willingdon and Sir William Vincent, been inserted at this entry. The large silver charger given by Lady Goldsborough in 1698 is placed within the font at the time of baptisms. The imposing picture over the altar is believed, though there is no actual proof, to have been taken from Pondicherry by the British when that possession was captured under Lord Pigot. It is held to have been executed by a pupil of Raphael. The objection has been raised that the condition of the picture does not warrant the assumption of any great antiquity, but this does not take into account the fact of the picture having been restored only a hundred years ago. At any rate the technique of the painting proves it to have been done by a master hand and in Raphael's style.

The altar rails were presented by a Princess of Tanjore; and the Lectern, of the same date and design, by Lady Hobart.

The Silver Plate is very fine, and has been augmented of late years by the addition of the old silver from Pulicat. Among the various pieces is (1) the alms-dish, given by Elihu Yale, Governor of Madras in 1687, and founder of Yale University, (2) a silver flagon, given by Lady Goldsborough and inscribed with her name and coat-of-arms, (3) the large silver dish already mentioned and given by the same donor as the above, (4) the chalice, formed partly of a candlestick (or crucifix?) taken from Pondicherry. The cup is probably of English and the cover of Indian manufacture. There are several other massive and handsome pieces of silver of ancient date which according to the custom of that age are not hall-marked.

The registers date from the opening of the Church for Divine service, and contain all the births, marriages and deaths from 1680 to the present time. The first register was damaged and a copy therefore made in 1739 by Alexander Wynch, which cost 50 pagodas. Among the many interesting entries are the baptism of Charnock's three daughters (already referred to), and that of David Yale, son of the Governor; the marriage of Robert Clive to Margaret Maskelyne on February 18, 1753, and the witnessing signature of the Duke of Wellington, who was then Colonel Arthur Wellesley and stationed in the Fort.

The Bible used by Sir Streynsham Master at the building of Saint Mary's was given to the Church by one of his descendants, and is kept for inspection with the other old books.

In this brief survey a description has been given only of the oldest *British* building in Madras, but, as before mentioned, there are older pieces of non-British architecture existing. These are chiefly associated with the ancient Portuguese city of San Thomé, with its adjacent city of Mylapore (Méliapore). Here, it is believed, the apostle Saint Thomas lived, and died near by at Saint Thomas' Mount, and there is a large amount of continuous evidence to support this belief. The original and the present cathedrals were built over the shrine of Saint Thomas, legendarily stated to be made of the wooden log dragged by Saint Thomas across the beach. This shrine is to be seen by visitors.

The oldest building of all in San Thomé is the Luz Church; an inset inscription records the fact that the Church was built in 1516, but there is some doubt as to whether this is the authentic date. It was certainly built by the middle of the sixteenth century, but the ancient Church of Saint Thomas at the Mount, raised in 1522, is perhaps the older of the two, and therefore the oldest European building on the Coast.

C. DE LA B.

## THE CITY AND CORPORATION OF MADRAS

THE area included within the municipal boundary of Madras is some twenty-seven square miles: the extreme length of the City from north to south is about nine miles, the greatest breadth at any one point about four miles.

The public affairs of the City are, and for long have been, administered by a Municipal Corporation. In the constitution of this body important changes were introduced by the Madras City Municipal Act of 1919, which came into operation on the first day of October in that year. By re-arrangement of internal boundaries the former twenty divisions of the City were increased to thirty, and each division returns a representative to the Council: 'Institutional bodies,' so called, return eleven members; such bodies are the two Chambers of Commerce, the Trades Association, the University of Madras and others: and the remaining nine members, who make up the number of the City

Fathers to fifty, are appointed by the Government of Madras. Under former Acts the President of the Corporation, who was at the same time the Corporation's Chief Executive Officer, was appointed by the Local Government: the new Corporation elects its own President, but the appointment of Chief Executive Officer, who is styled the 'Municipal Commissioner,' and who does not sit in the Council as a member, still rests with the Government. Every taxpayer enjoys the right of voting at elections.

It is the common lot of a municipal body to suffer abuse. Far from being an exception to this rule the Madras Corporation might find scriptural warrant for being puffed up on the score that all men, or at least, a good many men, daily speak ill of it. The critic of City affairs pays scant heed to what is done for his comfort, and in his expositions of what ought to be done disregards the trammels of financial possibility. Madras is, comparatively, a poor city; its revenue from all source during the year 1919–20 amounted to but Rs. 37·38 lakhs. This sum considered *per se* is not inconsiderable; but, in relation to the purposes, which it has to serve, it is woefully insufficient. Madras, geographically speaking, has not so much expanded as straggled; perhaps a more correct description would be that the municipal boundary line has been drawn so widely as to include quarters or outlying villages that have little real connection with the city proper. These outlying areas, sparsely populated for the most part, contribute little to the municipal coffers; while their remoteness renders their proper municipal service — roads, water, sanitation, lighting, etc. — disproportionately costly.

The figures of the last two decennial enumeration seem to indicate that Madras, in the matter of population, has about reached its limit of expansion. Between 1881 and 1901 more than 100,000 souls were added to the city: the succeeding ten years showed but an increase of 9,000, and the increase of the following decade was still more inconsiderable (4,291). To this last figure has still to be added 'the floating population,' which represents, in the main, those arriving in the port of Madras within a certain period of time after the census night; but even with this addition the final increase is likely to be inconsiderable.

Many explanations have been offered of this phenomenon. In the teeth of the Corporation is often cast the unhealthiness of the city; a fact deduced from the city's death-rate, which certainly at first sight compares unfavourably with the corresponding rates of Bombay and Calcutta. But in a mere comparison of figures, without regard to qualifying circumstances, there is little to be found save an opportunity for uninstructed fault-finding. The population of Madras is a thing essentially different from the populations of the two greater cities. In Madras there is a practical equality of the sexes. In Bombay and Calcutta an immense preponderance of males over females suggests irresistibly an influx of adult male labourers to the industries of these towns; and a population largely immigrant, whose continuance in a city is practically dependent on physical fitness for employment, is likely to be in healthier case than one which comprises the old of both sexes, and a fair proportion of children and infants. The birth-rate of Madras is far higher than that of Bombay and Calcutta; and in a poor Oriental city it is an undeniable, if regrettable, fact that infantile mortality is likely to rule high.

A consideration of probabilities reinforces the suggestion of the census figures. Madras, so far, has not discovered a fuel field within reasonable distance; the city's water supply, though sufficient for domestic uses, is quite inadequate for industrial operations on a large scale; the port, described by its creator as 'a challenge flaunted in the face of nature,' is not, and is scarcely likely to become, one of the great ports of the East. The ideal of the city should be not a greater aggregation of human beings, but a mere comfortable disposal of, and better provision for, those already living within the city's limits.

For the comparatively well-to-do Madras is probably a pleasanter place of residence than the wealthier, more modernized, and more 'Westernized' cities wherewith it is often compared. The transference to the East of Western speed, and Western economy of space, is a blessing attended with some disadvantages. Distances, when considered in relation to transport facilities, are preposterous in Madras; but there some compound or garden space is conceded as a necessary appendage to every decent dwelling: the flat overlooking a street is as yet practically unknown. It is not uninteresting to explain the increasing difficulty of finding bungalow accommodation, the marked rise in house-rents, by the theory that the European settler in the East has impressed his ideas of domestic comfort on the Indian. The wealthy Indian, who formerly lived in his Georgetown office buildings, and built a suburban bungalow for lease to a European, now occupies his own bungalow; the steadily growing desire for comfortable surroundings on the part of those who can afford them has raised the value of building land, and thereby rendered building for lease to others a comparatively unattractive investment. The real sufferers in point of residence in Madras are the clerks and the labourers. Under present conditions it is a practical impossibility to house decently, and on an economic basis either clerk or manual labourer within the city: plans for moving such without the city, which pay little regard to lack of transport, and to distances already existing within the city, are, one fears, vain and unrealizable. The clerk and labourer, or persons of equivalent financial position, constitute the majority of the city's inhabitants: till they are housed in comparative decency, Madras will not show a creditable bill of health. With wages, land prices, building costs, at this present level, such housing is impossible. Suggestions that the unhealthiness, the 'slave-mentality,' engendered by dwelling in pig-styes may be swept away by the discarding of clothes, are scarcely helpful.

An increase in earning capacity, or rather an increase in salaries and wages paid, does not seem immediately probable. The volume of business doable in Madras is, comparatively speaking, too small to endure greatly-increased overhead charges. If land values do not automatically fall, which seems unlikely, the only line of advance would appear to be by legislation of the kind ordinarily described as 'socialistic' in respect of land and housing. It is not advisable, in the interests of the community, that an individual should be allowed to cover his land with miserable, insanitary, hovels, and to draw profit therefrom; if he cannot find capital for the proper development of his land, it is scarcely right that, by claiming an exorbitant site price, he should preclude a public body from undertaking such development.

To abolish poverty, or to raise by rule or enactment the standard of life in a city, is beyond the present power of a Municipal Corporation. But in the provision for certain common needs of the citizens the Madras Corporation has some substantial achievement to its credit. Of these, the most important is the recent provision of drinking water. The source of supply, the Red Hills Lake, remains the same. Up to the year 1914 the method of supply was by an earthen channel from the lake to a deep masonry shaft, whence mains were laid into the city. The *maximum* supply possible by the method was about six and a half million gallons *per diem*. Works carried out by the Corporation at a cost of Rs. 55·62 lakhs have rendered it possible to maintain an average daily supply of about fifteen million gallons. Were the water at the source sufficient a distribution of twice this quantity would be perfectly feasible. But even as things are, the daily supply provides more than twenty-five gallons *per diem* per head of the population; and the supply is continuous.

Increased water-supply demands improved drainage facilities. In the matter of drainage, the Corporation's work, mainly owing to financial reasons, has been less complete. It is certainly less appreciated by the citizens. Water is a positive benefit; buildings make an insistent appeal to the eye. Drainage is negative; it is the removal of a nuisance, not the conferring of an amenity; and its efficient working, because underground and therefore out of sight, is generally out of mind. The public memory is short; many people, now living in clean dry streets, and grumbling at the payment of drainage tax, forget that but a few years ago black sluggish streams of sewage flowed visibly and odoriferously past their doorsteps.

The Corporation maintains about 300 miles of metalled road, and much of the mileage is of a very fair standard of excellence. Metal is supplied from the practically inexhaustible quarries of Pallaveram, which are worked directly by the Corporation. That a certain deterioration is observable of recent years can hardly be denied; but this deterioration is not attributable to neglect or incapacity. The Madras roads belong to the era of the horse drawn vehicle; with the coming of the motor the volume and speed-pressure of traffic have, for the time being, outstripped progress in the remodelling of roads to suit new conditions. In this there is nothing peculiar to Madras; most cities find themselves in similar case. An important advance has been made in the matter of lighting, which renders these roads safe for modern vehicular speed: the dingey old kerosene lamps, considered adequate twenty years ago, are rapidly being replaced by electric lighting.

A prophet is seldom held in honour in his own country : a Municipal Corporation must expect to serve the humble purpose of an Aunt Sally. The Corporation of Madras, if it sins, can hardly plead that it sins in ignorance. Yet the critic who day in and day out points to the things that the Corporation might do and yet does not do, who scoffs at the pointless loquacity of the Council meetings, might at times with profit reflect that there is another side to the shield. What the Corporation *can* do is limited by the amount of money at its disposal: the ratepayer, who clamours for better public services, should, if he were logical, accompany his clamour by the proffer of increased rates. If the Corporation be accused of useless talkings, it can retort with truth that, while it talks on but one afternoon of each month, it, on every day of the year, removes 350 tons of rubbish from the streets, supplies more than half a million persons with drinking water, carries away nine million gallons of sewage from human habitations, lights about seven thousand lamps, keeps in fair and safe order hundreds of miles of road.

J. C. M.

## MADRAS MUSEUM AND CONNEMARA PUBLIC LIBRARY

IN Pantheon Road, next to the Maternity Hospital, in a group of red brick buildings, is housed the Government Central Museum and Connemara Public Library. The ground floor of the building nearest the road, to the front of which the Museum Theatre is attached, is devoted on one side to pre-historic antiquities, and on the other to an interesting collection of old arms, mostly from the Madras Arsenal and Tanjore Armoury. Above is the Bruce Foote collection of pre-historic antiquities, a small gallery illustrative of the ethnology of the Presidency, and a large collection of South Indian metal ware, including household utensils, lamps, articles used in household and temple worship, and an exceptionally fine set of Hindu images together with a few Buddhist ones.

The next building contains the Connemara and University Libraries. The Oriental Manuscripts

Library, ultimately to be amalgamated with the latter, is at present housed in a small building right at the back of the Museum.

The third and last building contains the rest of the Museum collections, the centre and western side being devoted to zoology, the north wing to geology, and (at present) botany, and the east side to economic botany, and (at present) geology on the upper floor, and archæology on the ground floor. Special attention may be directed to the collections of South Indian birds and fishes, the former including several groups mounted with their nests in natural surroundings, the collection of timbers and building stones, the old hand painted and printed palampores at present temporarily housed in Economic gallery, and the fine collection of sculptures from the ancient Buddhist stupa at Amaravati on the bank of the Kistna river.

## VICTORIA INSTITUTE

Those who wish to purchase specimens of South Indian art will find a good collection magnificently housed, and well displayed, in the Victoria Institute, next door to the Museum. The exhibits include wood and ivory carving, furniture, gold, silver, brass and lacquer ware, carpets, mats, lace, embroidery, saris, toys, etc. All articles are on sale at moderate prices.

F. H. G.

## MADRAS HARBOUR

UNLIKE most of the ports of India, Madras possesses no vestige of a natural harbour, and before the present artificial one was built landing at Madras was an alarming, and sometimes dangerous, proceeding. Large open boats, known as masulah boats, made of planks tied together with rope, were used to bring passengers and luggage from ships, accompanied by small catamarans which rescued the passengers when, owing to insufficient bailing, or inconvenient breakers, the masulah boats sank or capsized.

The construction of the artificial harbour of Madras was commenced in June, 1875, and the two breakwaters forming the Harbour with 515 feet opening in the centre of the eastern side were nearly completed at the end of September, 1881. On November 12, 1881, a cyclone wrecked both the eastern breakwaters from the elbows to the entrance. The reconstruction of the damaged portions was started in July, 1884, and was completed on May 9, 1896.

**Between 1904 and 1910.**—The form of the artificial harbour was altered by the closing of the old eastern entrance and by the opening of a new entrance, 400 feet wide, at the north-eastern corner, protected by a massive breakwater 1,600 feet long with a 5,000 ton monolithic bastion block at its end. The protecting arm was commenced in July, 1906, the new entrance opened in January, 1910, and the old entrance closed in September, 1910; the work of alteration was completed in 1911. On the night of November 22-23, 1916, Madras Port was attacked by a violent cyclone with the result that the 5,000 ton monolith with about 130 feet of the sheltering arm behind was totally wrecked and buried in the sea, and another 100 feet of the arm was badly shaken. The restoration work was immediately started and is now approaching completion.

**Between 1904 and 1919** many other improvements were carried out. The chief amongst them are :—

*Between* 1904 *and* 1910—

(1) A nine-acre boat basin was excavated south of South Harbour arm for the accommodation of small craft from 1,000 tons downwards. The

sides were equipped with jetties and wharves and hydraulic cranes for the landing and shipping of iron and rough goods as well as for non-dutiable coasting cargo.

(2) To the south of this basin, connected to it by a canal, is a two-acre timber pond equipped with jetties, cranes, and all facilities for handling the timber trade for which a large storage area is reserved around the pond.

(3) A slipway at the north-west corner of the Boat basin capable of taking vessels up to 500 tons deadweight. Besides the slipway, there are three ramps on which smaller barges and boats are repaired.

(4) *Piers*—

(i) An export screw pile pier was constructed in 1905.

(ii) A dutiable import pier was constructed in 1907.

(iii) A non-dutiable import pier was constructed in 1909.

The above piers as well as the old ocean pier constructed in 1858 were dismantled between 1913 and 1916 to make way for the West Quay described below.

(5) *Transit Sheds.*—About 7½ acres of single storey first-class shedding have been constructed —four sheds along the whole length of the West Quay and one to the east of the Boat Basin—in addition to half-a-dozen small sheds.

*Between* 1910 *and* 1919—

(6) The construction of a granite quay, known as the West Quay, 3,000 feet long along the west face of the Harbour, for vessels of thirty feet draft and under to lie alongside, and work their cargo direct into the shore, was started in 1910 and completed in 1917. The quay can accommodate vessels of any length, normally four vessels are berthed at a time, and it is equipped with hydraulic cranes. Besides the West Quay there are—

(i) The South Quay—a strong steel wharf, 335 feet in length, thirty-two feet wide with thirty feet water alongside, capable of accommodating vessels up to 600 feet in length, on the north face of the south breakwater—constructed in 1911 and chiefly used by Rangoon and Singapore passenger vessels as well as by horse and cattle boats;

(ii) The East Quay, with twenty-six feet of water alongside, on the inner side of the closed entrance for working one vessel; normally used by coal steamers which discharge their cargo direct into waggons; and

(iii) an outer quay, also with twenty-six feet of water alongside, on the inner side of the north sheltering arm outside the new entrance used for the discharge of case oil.

(7) The construction—for the use of merchants as warehouses—of three double storey warehouses with a floor area of 4½ acres has been completed.

(8) Besides the sheds and warehouses, on the sea front, in the centre of the West Quay, has been constructed a fine two-storey stone face central office which accommodates the Direction, Accounts, Marine, and Traffic staff, with a central tower for the Port Signalling Establishment.

(9) A well-equipped workshop and a Hydraulic Power House have also been constructed at the root of the South Harbour arm.

A. K. W.

## PLACES AND OBJECTS OF HISTORICAL INTEREST AROUND MADRAS

VISITORS to Madras may like to know of the many places and objects of historical interest in the immediate vicinity of this Presidency town. The radius dealt with may appear at first sight somewhat extensive, but it should be remembered that these are the days of easy and expeditious travel, and therefore what might have been considered an impracticable journey for the purpose of such sight-seeing fifty, or even thirty years ago, is now considered part of a very easy day's work. It is perhaps for this reason that so little was formerly known of such places by the ordinary tourist, seeing that they are now only beginning to be brought within focus.

The environs of the City itself comprise the following:—

On the north, Perambur, and Ennur, distant from Madras some four, and thirteen miles respectively.

On the south, San Thomé, Adyar, and Saint Thomas' Mount.

On the west, Poonamallee.

Ennur has been for about a hundred and fifty years well known to the settlers in Madras as a health resort, and the old bungalows of the Company's magnates in the days of Clive are to be seen in use to-day. But although it is redolent with past traditions, Ennur is now only a holiday resort and has nothing of historical importance about it.

When we turn to San Thomé we find a more fruitful field of research. The Catholic Cathedral of Saint Thomas at Mylapore carries us back to the seventeenth century. There is to be seen the shrine of the reputed relics of Saint Thomas, and around the building itself was fought out the struggle for supremacy and Empire between the Portuguese, French, Dutch, and English. On the banks of the Adyar were fought those series of triumphs about 1746-8 by the gallant Paradis, who might be termed Dupleix's right-hand man at that time.

Saint Thomas' Mount is full of reminiscences of the conquest of South India by the English, and many relics of the civil and military vicissitudes of Madras are visible. Its occupation by

Hyder 'Ali is recalled by the sight of the gun emplacements and ring bolts for the heavy guns, placed there by Hyder in 1769. Traces of the famous 'Garden Houses' of the Governors and high officials of the Company are also still to be seen, some of them being actually inhabited to this day. Most people who have read the history of Madras, and have seen the nameless grave at the chancel steps of the Fort Church, will be interested in identifying Lord Pigot's house of detention at Saint Thomas' Mount. It is the corner-house of the Parade Ground next the present Indian Infantry Hospital.

The Mount has often been the centre of the struggle which from time to time raged round Madras, traces of which are to be seen to the south-west of the Cantonment, in the existing alignment of former entrenchments on the large maidan, where the golf links are to-day. What is there known, popularly, as 'Tippu's Nullah' is the site of the position taken up by the British forces when Hyder 'Ali threatened Madras in 1769. The existence of trenches can also be detected at Pallaveram, three miles to the south, where a military camp was originally situated and the 'Veteran Corps' was afterwards stationed. These trenches were probably the site of the position taken up by the English forces when Hyder again threatened Madras after the famous 'Baillie Disaster' in 1780.

Nineteen miles on the old military road to Trichinopoly, which runs through Pallaveram and Chingleput, will bring one to Vandalur, which contains the famous Captain Joseph Smith's private bungalow, and the ancient site of a rest and concentration camp, often referred to in military histories of the days of Clive. From Vandalur a road runs to Covelong, the scene of one of Clive's most famous exploits, in which he wrested the fort from a superior French force, and partly won his title of 'a heaven-born leader'. The ruins of this fort can still be seen, and the spot is one of great natural beauty also. The visitor to Covelong will do well before going there to read a full account of the taking of the fort by Clive in 1752.

Poonamallee, twelve miles to the south-west of Madras, is one of the oldest British cantonments, and is mentioned throughout the history of the Carnatic Wars. The present magnificent hospital and fine barracks stand on the site of the original fort. In the entrenchments (still visible round the hospital) the mutilated survivors of Hyder's vengeance were gathered in July, 1780, only to starve and die by hundreds. Here the first Highland regiment to land in India (the 73rd Highlanders) were cantoned, shortly before they marched to Conjeeveram in Sir Hector Munro's army, to take partl in the greatest disaster that up to that time had ever befallen British arms in India. Here, on his release from the dungeons of Seringapatam, came the famous Sir David Baird, of whose return Theodore Hook has written so graphically in his 'Life of General Sir David Baird'.

Chingleput, and even a little further afield will be found to be well within our scope. Chingleput possesses the ruins of one of the most important forts in the Carnatic, a fort which is closely connected with Clive's most famous exploits, and with other important incidents of the Carnatic Wars. Here Clive further established his reputation as a leader directly after the taking of Covelong. Here Preston held out, and did invaluable service to the English cause at the critical time of Lally's campaign. This witnessed the passing by of Lally's host on its march to besiege Madras in 1758-59, the 'passing by' being accounted now as one of

Lally's crucial mistakes. Hither came also Sir Hector Munro's army in pell-mell retreat after the 'Baillie Disaster'. And now? The old fort around which the tumult of war has raged so fiercely is still in a state of preservation, owing chiefly to the fact that within it are situated the Reformatory School and Government offices. We hope at least that the scenery around the fort, which no history has changed, will compensate the visitor for this bathos.

Chingleput is thirty-five miles on the main line from Madras to Trichinopoly and can be reached easily by motor-car from Madras within two hours. Within easy distance of it are Sadras, Carangooly (now spelt Karunghuze), Wallajabad, Conjeeveram and Pollilore. Each of these places is connected with the stirring events leading up to the British conquest of South India.

Sadras, sixteen miles by road from Chingleput, was originally a Dutch settlement, which was finally ceded to the British in 1818. It was acquired by Holland in the seventeenth century when the Dutch were making a serious bid for a footing in the East. During the Carnatic Wars it figured prominently, and was used from time to time as neutral territory for the purpose of negotiations on the part of the belligerents of the other nations. Here in 1754 was held the famous 'Conference at Sadras', between the French under Dupleix, and the English under Governor Saunders, which came to a sudden end on a quarrel about the authenticity of the documents produced by the parties concerned. When Lally was besieging Fort Saint George in 1758–9, English refugees from Madras gathered here, and Lally outraged the laws of neutrality by taking Sadras, because of the sympathetic action of the Dutch towards them. Near Sadras Preston's reconnaissance party captured an object of subsequent great interest to the world at large in the shape of Lally's famous letter of indictment of the Pondicherry Council, with which he carried on a continuous quarrel throughout his campaign. The old Dutch fort at Sadras still stands fairly intact, and contains a small cemetery in which are well preserved Dutch tombs dating back to 1670–80. A very picturesque place, the more so as it is on the sea.

To-day the traveller from Ceylon to Madras will stop at the tiny wayside station of Karunghuze, twelve miles, before reaching Chingleput. The

Railway runs actually through the formerly famous little fort of Carangooly, which frequently appears in the pages of the history of the Carnatic Wars. It may well be described as the *best battered fort* of the Carnatic, for it was taken and re-taken a hundred times, and was the scene of many Homeric deeds. The most famous incident in its history was its surrender to Coote's army in December, 1759, at the time when Lally's valiant efforts were well-nigh spent, and Wandiwash was already looming up. Coote was unable to obtain the surrender of the gallant little French garrison though he threatened to put it to the sword, when he finally captured it, but in the end, as time was precious to him, he was obliged to grant honourable terms to his honourable foe. Commanded by an Irishman in the service of the French king, they exacted perhaps even more than the ordinary honours of war! With the exuberance of desperation this immortal company came forth. Their colours having been shot away they hoisted a shirt. They improvised martial strains on country horns and other instruments of musick. With rusty firelocks at the slope, emaciated by famine, tattered and forlorn in appearance, the last French garrison of Carangooly marched south. Eyre Coote never forgave the little fort this flaunt, and in 1782, having again suffered from it at the hands of Hyder, he levelled it with the ground, for which he was severely reprimanded.

Wandiwash is not far from Carangooly, but too far perhaps to be considered within the scope of this article.

Wallajabad, about thirty-two miles from Madras, and fourteen miles from Chingleput, is now a worn-out cantonment, and has been for some time abandoned, but it contains many interesting marks of its former prosperity and importance. Some of the old military bungalows still stand inhabited. One of them, which is circular in shape, and has an interior covered with a fine pink polished chunam, is now the property of the Scotch Mission. The old parade grounds are still to be seen, and old sentry boxes stand facing the direction from which the hosts of Hyder were wont to come. A large crowded cemetery witnesses to the reputation for unhealthiness which this station once bore. It was at Wallajabad that Baird commanded after the capture of Seringapatam, and here that he wrote his letters of protest, which resulted in his regiment being broken up and drafted into the 71st. Wallajabad was a scene of disaffection at the time of the Vellore Mutiny in 1806, and some of the Indian troops suffered here the extreme penalty then meted out to mutineers. Traces of the famous Wallajabad race course are yet to be seen. The Palar River runs beside the town, and the scenery is very picturesque there in the cold season.

Conjeeveram is only six miles from Wallajabad and is worth a visit. The Great Pagoda has been the scene of many military operations. In 1758–9 Lally occupied it, and Draper's force took it before the battle of Wandiwash. In 1780 Munro's force occupied and fortified it in the presence of Hyder's huge host encamped close by at Muserawaukam. In the tank of the temple still lie Munro's heavy ordnance, which he abandoned and sank there after Baillie's defeat.

Nine miles to the north-east of Conjeeveram is Pollilore, the scene of Baillie's disaster, which is accounted one of the greatest disasters to the British arms in India. It took place on September 6th–10th 1780, and is referred to once or twice above in these pages. The story can be read in any Indian history. It has become famous in the history of heroic deeds of the Empire owing to the great bravery and discipline shown by the British troops, European and Indian alike. Baillie's famous 'last stand' was made close to the village of Pollilore, where his last 500 men without ammunition repelled thirteen attacks of Hyder's army of 86,000 men before finally surrendering. The few hundred survivors, included Sir David Baird who was marched, wounded as he was, with many others to Seringapatam fortress, to undergo there two and a half years of cruel captivity. The country at Pollilore remains as it was when the disaster took place, and one can gather yet from the inhabitants many interesting traditions of the battle. Relics of the fight are still obtainable, not the least interesting being broken Flemish pottery, which originally formed part of the crockery carried then by every individual officer.

We might carry the reader even further afield, for two other places may be included as within reach at the present day. Wandiwash, the scene of the battle bearing its name now accounted one of the decisive battles of the world, is only eighteen miles from Conjeeveram, while the great fortress of Ginjee is only twenty-five miles beyond Wandiwash.

We have, however, kept within a forty-mile radius, to bring the reader within touch of what might be described as 'Objects and Places of Historical Interest in the Vicinity of the City of Madras'.

E. B.

## GENERAL EDUCATION IN MADRAS

IN the City of Madras there are six first-grade colleges affiliated to the University—the Government Presidency College, the Government Muhammadan College, the Madras Christian College, the Pachaiyappa's College, the Government Queen Mary's College and the Women's Christian College. There is one second-grade college in Madras, viz. the Wesley College. The Presidency College is affiliated in Honours in English Language and Literature History and Economics, Mental and Moral Science, Sanskrit, Mathematics, Physics, Chemistry and Natural Science. The Christian College is affiliated in Honours in Mathematics, Physics, History and Economics, Sanskrit, English Language and Literature, Natural Science and Mental and Moral Science. The total number of students for Honours in the two colleges in the several classes is approximately 330. In addition to the tuition given to the Honours students in the individual colleges, there is a system of inter-collegiate lectures between the Presidency and the Christian Colleges. The system has produced satisfactory results and will, in all probability, be extended. Honours students also attend the University lectures given by the University Professors of Economics and Indian History. The progress of women's education may be measured by the fact that, though prior to 1915 there was no college for women in Madras affiliated to the University, the number of women now reading in the two women's colleges in Madras is approximately 300. In addition to this, twenty women are reading for Honours in the Presidency College. The Women's Christian College is under the control of a Council composed of the representatives of British and American bodies. There are also in Madras the Law College, the Medical College, the College of Engineering, Guindy, and the Teachers' College, Saidapet, all affiliated to the University. In the Law College courses are provided for three classes, the M.L., B.L., and the Pleadership. The total number of students in the three classes last year was 568. In the Engineering College courses are provided for three classes, the Bachelor of Civil Engineering class, the Upper Subordinate class and the Lower Subordinate class.

The course for the Engineering class extends over five years, of which four years are spent in the college and one year in workshops or on engineering works. The number of students in the college last year was 453. The Upper Subordinate class is being discontinued consequent on the re-organization of the Public Works Department. In 1920 the college reopened at Guindy in the new buildings which were started in 1914, and which not only provide increased accommodation and laboratory and workshop facilities but also enable the college to be wholly residential. At the Teachers' College, Saidapet, courses are provided for the L.T. class, the Secondary Grade Training class, the Manual Training class and the Gymnastic class. The total number of students on the rolls last year was 108. Hostels are attached to the following colleges :—The Presidency College, the Christian College, the Pachaiyappa's College, the Muhammadan College, the Medical College, the Engineering College, the Teachers' College and the Wesley College. Both the Women's Colleges are residential.

There are in Madras City thirty-one secondary schools for boys, and twenty secondary schools for girls, 280 elementary schools for boys, and sixty-eight elementary schools for girls. These figures include European schools. In addition to the above institutions, mention may be made of the Veterinary College, the Arts School, the Madras Trades School, the Leather Trades School, the Government Institute of Commerce and the Royapuram Medical School. The number of students in the Veterinary College last year was eighty-eight, and 2,932 cases were treated in the college hospital. The number of students in the Arts School last year was 241, including twenty-four women. Instruction is given in wood-work, carpet-weaving, metal work, jewellery, modelling, engraving, lacquer work and painting. The Government Trades School, Madras, which was started in 1916 as an experimental school of afternoon classes for apprentices engaged in the engineering and plumbing trades, has now more than 250 students studying mechanical engineering, electric wiring, plumbing, minor sanitary science, practical mathematics, machine drawing and wood-work. The Leather Trades Institute was opened in 1915, and is run partly as a model tannery and school, and partly as a research institute. The course extends over three years. The number of students under instruction last year was thirty-four. The Government Institute of Commerce works in two sections — the Audit class and the Technical Examination class — and last year the strength of the two classes was forty-five and eighty-one respectively. Instruction is given in accountancy, book-keeping, correspondence, geography, shorthand and banking.

There are in Madras City two Sanskrit Colleges — the Cunnan Chetti Sanskrit College, Triplicane, and the Madras Sanskrit College, Mylapore—each has a hostel attached. Tuition and boarding are free.

The Students' University Club opened in 1919 by His Excellency Lord Pentland now has a membership of over 200.

H. S. D.

## MEDICAL EDUCATION IN MADRAS

THE Madras Medical School, the precursor of the Medical College, was built and opened in July, 1836. The School, which was founded with the purpose of supplying Assistant Surgeons and Hospital Assistants for the Army, then consisted of only four departments, a Lecture Theatre, a library, a museum and a Laboratory. Private students were admitted two years later. In 1851 the Medical School became a College, and in 1877 was affiliated to the University of Madras, undertaking not only the training of Army Assistant Surgeons, but also students for the L.M. and S. and M.B. and B.S. degrees of the University of Madras.

The College has gradually continued to grow in all its departments, and alterations and additions have been made from time to time. The most important recent additions being the block composing the physiological, hygiene and bacteriological laboratories, which was opened in 1911, and the building erected in 1917 for the Biology and Physics classes. Owing to the fact that no buildings are allowed to be erected on the military zone, the Biology and Physics Laboratory could not be built in the Medical College grounds, and the General Hospital compound had, therefore, to be encroached upon. The staff of the College consists of thirteen Professors, two Lecturers, twenty-four Assistants to Professors and twelve Demonstrators. There are at present seven separate departments in the College, three of which are for the purpose of training Post-Graduates. These are—

(1) *The Military Assistant Surgeon Department,* also called the Apothecary Department, which consists of Military Assistant Surgeon pupils and of women students, whose educational qualifications are not sufficient to enable them, to take a University degree. On completion of their course these students are examined by and receive diplomas from the Board of Examiners in Medicine.

There are now eighty-seven students in all in this department, fifty-five military pupils and thirty-two lady students.

(2) *The College Department.*—This is composed of students, both men and women, studying for the

degrees of L.M. and S. and M.B. and B.S. of the Madras University, and comprises the great majority of students, the College containing at the present time 409, of whom thirty-one are lady students.

(3) *The Sanitary Department.*—This is for the purpose of training Sanitary Inspectors, a special class of them being formed annually.

(4) *The Chemist and Druggists Department,* which has been founded with a view to supplying well-qualified Chemists and Druggists for the Presidency. The students attending undergo a two years' course, at the termination of which they are required to pass the Government Technical Examination in Pharmacy.

*The Post-Graduate Departments are*—

(1) *The Assistant Surgeons' Post-Graduate Department,* a post-graduate class being formed annually for the benefit of Assistant Surgeons and Sub-Assistant Surgeons. The course consists mainly of clinical and practical demonstrations in Medicine, Tropical Medicine, Surgery, Midwifery, Ophthalmology and Pathology, including *post-mortem* examinations.

(2) *The Health Officers' Department,* in which post-graduates undergo a special course of training

on the lines of the D.P.H. courses held in Great Britain. At the end of the course the candidates are encouraged to appear for the B.S.Sc. (Bachelor of Sanitary Science) degree of the University of Madras which is recognized as a qualification for first-class health officers.

(3) *The Dental Department.*—This department, which has recently been established, is intended for special instruction in dentistry of qualified medical men, and for the training of private students who intend to proceed to Europe and obtain a diploma in Dentistry.

The number of students in the College has been steadily progressing for years past, and the total number of students on the rolls for 1920 to 1921 was 579. The College has, however, reached its limit of capacity and any further increase in the number of students will necessitate extensive additions to the College buildings. A new Pathological Block has been designed and sanctioned, but its construction is held in abeyance, as it is proposed to erect a new Medical College, and a much-needed new General Hospital on the Spur Tank. The students of the Medical College obtain clinical instruction at the Government General Hospital, the Maternity Hospital, the Ophthalmic Hospital, and the Lunatic Asylum. The Government Maternity and the Ophthalmic Hospitals are both well-equipped up-to-date hospitals, but the General Hospital is sadly lacking in the requisites of a modern General Hospital. As it is, however, recognized that the present General Hospital cannot be converted into a satisfactory modern hospital, a new hospital has been designed, and will, it is hoped, be erected on the Spur Tank site within the course of the next few years.

The Madras Medical College, although the leading institution for medical education in the Presidency, is not the only one, even in the City of Madras, for the Royapuram Medical School now undertakes the training of Sub-Assistant Surgeon pupils. Hospital Assistants, as they were then called, were originally trained at the Medical College, but in 1903 they were finally transferred to Royapuram. The Royapuram Medical School, which is entirely devoted to the medical education of Sub-Assistant Surgeon pupils, both military and civil, now has a staff of eleven Lecturers, and eleven Assistant Lecturers, and has about 550s tudents. The clinical instruction for these students was at one time only obtainable at the Native Infirmary which contained seventy-five beds, and at the Rajah Sir Ramaswami Mudaliar Lying-in Hospital, both of which adjoin the Medical School. Recently, however, an excellent hospital—the Government Royapuram Hospital—has been erected on the site of the old Monegar Choultry Hospital, and as this new hospital contains 350 beds and is fully equipped on modern lines, there is ample provision for the clinical instruction of students of the Royapuram Medical School. These students are examined by the Board of Examiners, and on passing the final examination are awarded the diploma of L.M.P., 'Licensed Medical Practitioner'.

In addition to the Royapuram Medical School, there are four other Medical Schools devoted to the training of Sub-Assistant Surgeon pupils, situated in the Presidency, one each at Tanjore, Vizagapatam, Madura and Calicut, whilst at Vellore, the Mission Medical School has been opened with the purpose of training women students for the L.M.P.

The number of lady students, especially Indian ladies, for medical qualification at the Medical College, Madras, and the Mission Medical School, has considerably increased during the last few years, whilst the total applications of all classes of students for admission to the Medical College, Madras, far exceeds the number that can be admitted annually. The Indian public is, therefore, apparently learning to recognize the value of a Western medical education.

F. F. E.

## THE KING INSTITUTE OF PREVENTIVE MEDICINE

THE King Institute, situated at Guindy about six miles from Madras, is named after Colonel King, C.I.E., I.M.S., late Sanitary Commissioner, Madras, who was chiefly responsible for its inception and was opened in 1903 by the then Governor, His Excellency Lord Ampthill. It was originally designed as a lymph depot for the supply of vaccine lymph to the Madras Presidency. Its activities have, however, extended considerably since that time, and it is now one of the three large Provincial Laboratories in India, functioning as the central vaccine lymph depot, the Provincial Bacteriological Laboratory and the Public Health Laboratory for the Presidency.

It is at present divided into two sections: one, the Vaccine Section dealing with the manufacture of calf lymph for vaccination against small-pox; and the other, the Microbiological Section, which undertakes the laboratory side of medical diagnosis and treatment, and also public health work.

The main building houses the Microbiological Section. The Vaccine Section is more scattered and consists of a series of yards and sheds for the calves together with an operation room, loading room, packing room, and other administrative buildings.

The Institute has its own water supply, lighting, and sewage systems, and also runs a large refrigerating plant for the storage of vaccine lymph, bacterial vaccines, sera and other perishable medical and veterinary supplies.

Connected with the public health side is a series of experimental filters for water purification. The system consists of three storage tanks, two small sand filters, and two mechanical filters (Jewell and Paterson) with appropriate pumps and connections.

The vaccine lymph section manufactures and issues over two million doses of lymph annually. This is distributed chiefly to the Civil Department in the Madras Presidency. Supplies are also made, however, to the Military authorities in Southern India, French India, and, to a certain extent, to Ceylon. During the late war large quantities of lymph was sent overseas to the troops operating in East Africa. The lymph manufactured at present is chiefly diluted with lanoline, but glycerin lymph is also available for supply.

The Microbiological Section is responsible for all clinical diagnosis of a bacteriological nature required by the various medical institutions in the Presidency, including the big hospitals in Madras. Bacterial vaccines, both curative and prophylactic, are manufactured in large quantities for all Government institutions and for the medical public at large. In 1919, in response to an appeal from the Government of India, the Section commenced the manufacture of anti-influenza vaccine on a large scale, and undertook to supply the Madras Presidency and also the southern army in the event of another serious outbreak of the disease.

Anti-cholera, and anti-typhoid and paratyphoid vaccines are prepared in the same way, and are issued at very low cost to the general public to encourage this form of protection from disease.

The examination and investigation of water supplies has always been a prominent feature of the work carried out at the King Institute. During the course of each year samples of water from every protected water supply, whether belonging to municipalities, railways, or jails, are collected by the Institute sample-takers, brought to the Institute, and examined. Samples from any proposed source of supply are also submitted for opinion and report. The Section has also been responsible for the majority of the experiments carried out with the experimental filters under the direction of the Committee on water purification, of which the Director of the Institute is the Secretary. Reports of these experiments have been made to the Medical Research Section of the Congress from time to time.

The King Institute has a good record of original work done by Officers while working on its staff. Colonel King was, and still is, one of the leading authorities on modern methods of vaccine lymph production.

The protozoological researches of Captain (now Major) Christophers while Superintendent are well known.

Medical Entomology has formed a very fruitful field for research in the hands of Major Patton and Cragg, who worked in collaboration at the Institute for some considerable time. The experience gained by these Officers culminated in the publication of their well-known textbook on Medical Entomology.

The Institute was the head-quarters of the Kala-Azar Commission in Madras in 1912. As the result of his work on this Commission, Major Patton formed the opinion that the disease was transmitted by the bed bug, a theory which has lately received considerable impetus by the discovery of a series of developmental stages in that insect by Mrs. Adie in Assam.

The interest which has always been taken in problems connected with water purification originated with the work done by Major (now Lieut.-Colonel) Clemesha while Sanitary Commissioner in Madras. The results of his researches on tropical standards of purity were published in many of the reports issued from the Institute, and formed the subject-matter of his book on 'Water Supplies in the Tropics'.

The staff of the King Institute will be 'At Home' to members of the Congress on Tuesday, January 31, from 4 to 6 p.m. when they will be very pleased to show visitors over the Institute, and demonstrate the work which is being carried on there.

J. C.

## NOTE ON THE MADRAS CITY WATERWORKS

*Sources of Supply.*—The Madras City water-supply forms part of a project undertaken with the object of utilizing, to the fullest economical extent, the waters of the Corteliar River and its tributaries. This is effected by means of a masonry weir built across the Corteliar River at Tamarapakkam, about seventeen miles north-west of Madras. The weir diverts the river—excluding the greater flood discharges—into a channel leading to the Cholavaram and Red Hills storage lakes, which also receive a considerable supply from the catchment areas that drain directly to them and to the supply channel.

From the lower lake, the Red Hills lake, is drawn the Madras City water-supply. The water from both lakes is also used to irrigate rice lands with a first crop area of 7,500 acres, and a second crop area of 3,200 acres. The water thus used for irrigation is about twice the present water-supply to Madras.

*Catchment Area and its Yield.*—The catchment areas of the system are as follows:—

| | | SQ. MILES |
|---|---|---|
| River Corteliar, Tirutani and Nagari above Tamarapakkam Anicut | ... | 1,105 |
| Red Hills Lake .. | ... | 23 |
| Cholavaram Lake ... | ... | 11 |
| Katankal River ... ... | ... | 62 |
| Boosikal River ... ... | ... | 44 |
| Total | ... | 1,245 |
| *Deduct*—Catchment area of River Corteliar above Kesavaram Anicut diverted into River Cooum | ... | 268 |
| Net catchment area | ... | 977 |

The average available yield is estimated at 4,320 million cubic feet per annum.

The capacities of the two lakes are:—

| | | | | |
|---|---|---|---|---|
| Red Hills Lake | ... | 2,162 | million cubic | feet. |
| Cholavaram Lake | ... | 579 | " | " |
| Total | ... | 2,741 | " | " |

*New Works.*—The works have been designed to supply a population of 6,60,000 with twenty-five gallons per head per day. They divide themselves naturally into two divisions:—

(1) The MAIN WORKS, which convey, filter, pump and deliver the water in bulk under pressure within the municipal boundary.

(2) The DISTRIBUTION WORKS, which distribute to the individual consumer the water delivered to the city in bulk by the Main Works.

These two divisions will be considered separately.

## MAIN WORKS

*Intake Tower.*—The tower is situated about 110 feet from the inner face of the top of the bund, to which it is connected by a steel footbridge. The inlets from the lake are at three different levels, and are provided with valves actuated by machinery inside the tower; by this means the purest water, which experiment shows is about five feet below the surface, can be drawn off whatever the level of the lake may be.

The tower has been built at a point where the lake is deep, so that in times of draught water can be drawn off to the lowest possible level.

*Screening Chamber and Roughing Filter.*—Two 24-inch pipes from the Intake Tower pass under the tank bund, and terminate in a screening chamber.

The walls of the screening chamber are fitted with moveable copper gauze screens, 3/32-inch mesh, having a total area of 125 square feet, through which the water must pass in order to reach the roughing filter.

After leaving the screening chamber, the water enters the roughing filter—a chamber 150 ft. × 108 ft. wide divided by a central wall—at floor level, and rises through a filtering medium, consisting of broken stone supported by stone slabs, which rest on brick piers. It then flows over a measuring weir into the conduit. The quantity of water flowing over the measuring weir is automatically recorded on a diagram attached to a drum actuated by an eight-day clock. The head is translated into flow by means of a 'Hutchinson' recorder. Two bye-passes are provided, so that the water can be passed directly into the conduit without filtration, should the surface of the lake sink below the level required to pass the full supply over the measuring weir.

The screening chamber and roughing filter are surrounded by a brick wall, three feet high, to keep out animals, leaves and other materials which would otherwise find their way into the water.

At present the roughing filter is out of use pending the results of experiments on the purification of the water supply.

*The Conduit.*—The conduit, which conveys the water from the roughing filter at Red Hills to the sand filters at Kilpauk, is a culvert seven miles long, with an average gradient of 1 in 4,470.

The brickwork and concrete were constructed with cement mortar in some special lengths, and where large quantities of water were encountered. In all other cases, a special mortar, called 'Combination Mortar,' was employed in the conduit and throughout the waterworks.

The whole of the internal surfaces of the conduit were coated with Portland cement plaster (one cement to three sand), $\frac{3}{4}$-inch thick, and the outside of the arch is plastered with $\frac{3}{4}$-inch of combination mortar.

*Filters.*—In all, twenty-one filters of the ordinary slow sand type were designed. Of these fourteen have been constructed, arranged in two rows of seven each, the intention being that six filters of each row—twelve in all—should always be in operation, allowance being made for one filter in each seven to be out of use for cleaning or repairs.

Owing to the economies necessitated by the war, the construction of the remaining seven filters was postponed and has only recently been started. The conduit which brings the water from the Red Hills is continued round the fourteen filters, and is connected to each bed by a 14-inch diameter cast-iron pipe, controlled by a valve, so that any filter may be isolated for cleaning or repair. Between the two rows of filters runs the filtered water conduit, to which filtered water is delivered separately from each bed. Each filter is 200 feet long and 100 feet wide, this being a convenient size for cleaning without throwing out of use too large a filter area at a time.

Below the top-of-sand level, the walls are slightly battered on the inside, in order that the sand, by its own weight, may be packed tightly against the walls, and thus prevent the free passage of water between the sand and the walls. As a further precaution against this 'water-creep' both the drains and the broken stone at the bottom of the filters are stopped three feet away from the walls; broken stone is placed round the ends of the drains and the space between the stone and the walls is filled with sand.

*Filtering Materials and Drains.*—The filtering materials consist of clean siliceous river sand, twenty-eight inches deep, screened to eliminate as nearly as practicable all material except that which passes through $\frac{1}{30}$-inch mesh and is retained on $\frac{1}{80}$-inch mesh.

Under the fine sand layer is a layer of coarse sand, two inches deep, resting on broken granite laid in two layers, each two inches deep. The coarse sand is screened so that its grains will pass $\frac{1}{8}$-inch mesh sieve and be retained on a $\frac{1}{30}$-inch mesh sieve. The top layer of stone will pass a $\frac{3}{8}$-inch ring and be retained on a $\frac{1}{8}$-inch ring. The bottom layer will pass a $\frac{3}{4}$-inch ring and be retained on a $\frac{3}{8}$-inch ring.

Below the bottom layer of broken stone are the brick drains consisting of two layers of best pressed bricks laid flat. The main drain is semi-circular, twenty-four inches wide, and is covered by stone slabs two inches thick.

*Filter Outlet Regulator.*—The main drain leads to the rectangular Filter Outlet Chamber, which contains a Glenfield-Jones Automatic Outlet Regulator, the object of which is to maintain a constant rate of filtration.

*Filtered Water Tanks.*—The filtered water flows into three underground covered tanks, each 150 feet square and with a depth of ten feet of water having a capacity of 1,400,000 gallons.

The floor consists of two feet of concrete in combination mortar. The side walls are of brickwork in combination mortar rendered on the inside faces with cement plaster. The roof consists of brick jack arches springing from steel girders, supported on brick cross walls, which are carried by arches springing from granite piers. Access to each tank is provided by means of manholes. Vent pipes provide inlets and outlets for the air which continually enters and leaves the tanks as the water level falls and rises.

Each tank is provided with inlet and outlet pipes. Both are thirty inches in diameter, and are fitted with sluice valves so that any tank may readily be isolated for cleaning or repairs without interfering with the working of the other tanks. A scour is also provided for each tank.

*Pumping Station.*—From the pure water tanks the water gravitates to the pumping station suction culvert, whence it is pumped into the Corporation mains, an elevated tank being connected with the pumping main to act as a balancing tank between the pumps and the distribution system.

The Pumping Plant was supplied and erected by Messrs. James Simpson and Co. It comprises three High Duty Direct Acting Worthington engines and pumps, each capable of delivering 12,000 gallons of water per minute against a maximum total head of eighty feet including suction. Three Babcock and Wilcox boilers are provided, each able to supply steam continuously to any two engines working together, and delivering the maximum discharge against the maximum head.

A Venturi meter is inserted on the forty-eight inch main into which the pumps discharge. It will register flows up to 1,800,000 gallons per hour. A combined water level and pump pressure recorder is also provided, so that complete records are available for calculating the work done by the plant.

*Elevated Steel Tank.*—An elevated steel tank has been provided to maintain a balance between the water pumped and the constantly varying demand for the city.

The tank is circular in plan, 104 feet in diameter, and twenty-eight feet deep from overflow level to the flat bottom. It has a capacity of one and a half million gallons. In order to maintain an adequate pressure all over the city, the tank has been designed with its floor fifty-eight feet, and top water eighty-six feet, above mean sea level. The ground level of Madras varies from eight to twenty, with a mean of about twelve feet above mean sea level.

The tank is built of steel throughout and is covered by a steel roof. An overflow has been provided, consisting of a pipe thirty-six inches in diameter, running vertically up the centre of the tank, and arranged to act also as a support for the roof. Only a small proportion of water supplied to the city actually passes through the tank, and therefore one pipe is sufficient to act as both inlet and outlet. It takes the form of a thirty-six inch diameter steel pipe branching off the forty-eight inch pumping main.

*Tank Supports.*—The tank is supported by an external ring of brick piers and arches, while steel stanchions, surrounded with brickwork, are used for the central supports, in order to minimise the weight, which, if only brick supports were used, would be excessive.

The area of exposed metal has been reduced to a minimum. The upper surfaces of the floor beam casings, which constitute the actual support for floor of the tank, are in the form of long flat tablings separated by channels. The floor plates of the tank are arranged so that their longitudinal points come over the centres of the concrete channels. This enabled the plates to be riveted up without difficulty. As a protection against corrosion, the bottom of the tank itself has been coated with cement plaster one inch thick.

*Pumping Main.*—A steel main, about 3,000 feet long, conveys the water from the main works to the distribution system. It is constructed of steel pipes, $\frac{7}{16}$-inch thickness, each of which is twenty-five feet long. The joints are made with double steel collars run solid with lead. The deviations from straight line are made in the joints, except in the vertical joints, where bevelled collars are used.

*Distribution System.*—The distribution system has been designed to supply twenty-five gallons of water per head per day and at this rate to provide a pressure of fifty feet above ground level at the ends of the principal mains. As a matter of fact, in order to reduce waste, the valves on the principal mains are partially closed and the full pressure is not maintained at any time of the day.

*Minimum Size of Pipe.*—The smallest new pipe is four inches in diameter. Owing to the expense of replacing all the existing 3-inch by 4-inch pipes, it was decided to retain the old pipes wherever they are not too small to supply domestic requirements. In Madras 3-inch pipes very quickly become choked with incrustations and sediment, and require frequent cleaning; they are also quite inadequate for fire-extinguishing purposes.

*Purification of Water Supply.*—The sand filters have been found to work well, but there are occasionally breakdowns when purification is not satisfactory. In view of inevitable contamination of the Red Hills water, and the impossibility of removing all disease germs by any sand filter, however perfect, Major-General Giffard, in consultation with Major J. Cunningham and Major J. Morrison, recommended that the work of sand filters should be supplemented by chlorination. Before chlorination is finally adopted, it is necessary to decide the form in which chlorine should be applied—the point of application, dose and form of application. In order to determine these points, the Madras Corporation have obtained an experimental chlorinating plant capable of producing 15½ lbs. of available chlorine per day and are applying it to the water in pre-determined doses. If, as a result of the experiments, chlorination is adopted to destroy bacteria, the proper function of the filters will be to clarify the water, and experiments are now being made to determine how this can be done most economically. It is thought that smaller and therefore cheaper filters may be obtained by reducing the thickness of the filtering layers, and increasing the rate of filtration. Experiments on these lines are now in progress at Kilpauk and may be inspected by the members of the Congress when they visit the Kilpauk Water Works.

(See also the article on 'The Chlorination of Water Supplies' by Major J. Cunningham, pp. 90–94.)

J. W. M.

# THE CHLORINATION OF WATER SUPPLIES

CHLORINATION as a means of sterilizing drinking water was practically unknown twenty years ago. It is now one of the most valuable means we have at our disposal for this purpose. The evolution of the process forms an interesting chapter in Sanitary History.

Introduced primarily as a disinfectant for sewage it was first utilized, as far as water supplies are concerned, to disinfect specifically infected distribution systems. The idea of its systematic use for water purification appears to have first taken shape in the opening years of the present century. Nesfield in this country recommended 'chlorination' as a method applicable to active service conditions. Houstan and MacGowan in England, and Johnston and Leal in America, first attempted its use as a routine for large water supplies.

Two schools of thought would appear to have

arisen with regard to the correct manner of its application.

The first, represented by the European countries and especially the Germans, aimed at a very high standard of purification after a short period of contact. Here sterilization was attempted by the addition of large quantities of the active principle followed by the addition of suitable re-agents designed to effect its removal by chemical action.

The second school, represented chiefly by the Americans, attempted to attain the same object by the use of minimal doses of chemical allowed to act over longer periods of time without any subsequent treatment.

The latter method is now the one universally advocated. The excessively high standards demanded in European countries were found to be unnecessary in practice, and the opposition of public opinion to any 'doping' of the drinking water militated against the introduction of a system which sometimes made itself apparent by leaving the purified water with a disagreeable taste. The advent of the last war together with the altered conditions which followed in its train further popularized the method. The success which attended the chemical treatment of the water issued to large bodies of troops in the field together with the greatly increased cost of keeping up the huge plants required for large cities, forced the responsible authorities to consider cheaper methods of purification for large scale operations as a set-off to necessary increases in their plant. Thus, London, in 1916, commenced to chlorinate a portion of its supply, and in the following year treated most of its water in this way. In America, in 1918, it was estimated that over 1,000 cities were employing the process, and over 3,000 million gallons of water were being treated daily.

In India, where sanitation is chiefly conspicuous by its absence, and where an uncontaminated water-supply is almost unknown, chlorination would appear to be especially applicable. It was first used on a large scale at Poona as a result of an investigation into seasonal diarrhœa carried out by Major J. Morrison, I.M.S. The results have been eminently satisfactory.

As a result of a visit paid by Major Morrison to Madras, the Committee on Water Purification, in conjunction with the Madras Corporation, have decided to test the applicability of the method to the Madras City water supply, and through it to other supplies in the Presidency. A small chlorination plant and some filters for some experimental work are in the process of erection at the Madras Corporation Water Works at Kilpauk, and will soon be ready for use. The experiments, if successful, should ensure to the city of Madras a greatly increased supply of pure water at a much smaller capital cost than would be possible were the same results to be attempted by slow sand filtration alone.

Three methods of producing chlorine for water purification may be considered from the practical point of view :—

(1) The addition of 'Bleach solution' or hypochlorite of lime which should contain about 33 per cent of available chlorine.

(2) Chlorine gas (100 per cent value) obtainable in cylinders in liquid form.

(3) Electrolytic hypochlorite solution obtained by the electrolysis of salt (sea water, brine, etc.).

The choice of method depends to a great extent upon the water supply to be chlorinated.

Bleaching powder was the chief re-agent used for the troops on active service, and is of most value in small operations. For large water supplies one of the two latter methods is preferable. The addition of pure chlorine gas from cylinders has much to recommend it on the score of cost and simplicity, but the difficulty of obtaining the gas cylinders in India is a serious disadvantage. For a large city like Madras, and especially for an experimental plant, the electrolytic method is eminently suitable under the conditions at present prevailing. The Madras Corporation have ordered a plant of this type, and the experiments to be carried out at Kilpauk will be conducted with chlorine produced in this way.

J. C.

# PRE-HISTORIC ARCHÆOLOGY IN MADRAS

THE pre-historic archæology of South India is represented by (I) a Palæolithic Age, (II) a Neolithic Age, and (III) an Early Iron Age. The peculiarities of the South Indian sequence are—(1) that the culture of the later Palæolithic period (corresponding to the Aurignacian, Solutrian and Magdalenian[1] phases of Western Europe) is absent, and (2) that the Neolithic culture appears to pass directly into the Iron Age without the intervention of a period when copper or bronze was the staple material for weapons and implements.

The sequence of cultures cannot be tested by stratigraphical evidence or associated fauna or flora, and no human skeletal remains have been found which can be definitely assigned to either the Palæolithic or Neolithic Age, but the types of material found, the material used and its treatment suffice to differentiate these cultures beyond dispute.

[1] The evidence of the Kurnool caves is indeterminate.

I. The classic area of Palæolithic culture lies in the Districts of Chingleput, North Arcot and Chittoor, within a radius of about forty-five miles of Madras. A similar culture exists in the north of Nellore District and in the adjoining area of Kurnool. It can be traced along the middle Godavari right across India to the Indus. A few isolated finds are reported from Tanjore, Madura Tinnevelly, and Bellary, but there is no trace of any large settlement south of the Madras area. Palæolithic man chipped his implements from the big quartzite pebbles of the lateritic conglomerate overlying the Cuddalore sand-stones in the Chingleput and Nellore areas. In form these implements resemble the Chellean and Acheulean types of the early Palæolithic age of Western Europe, types which are found abundantly in Somaliland and also (sparingly) in Egypt and South Africa. Commonest are the 'bouchers' or 'coups de poing,' oval or pyriform, and of wonderful symmetry, and discoid stones, the use of which is doubtful. Distinctive of Madras are hatchet-like celts with square or oblique edge, the latter well described as the 'guillotine' type.

II. Neolithic man, on the other hand, fashioned

his celts almost without exception from 'trap' rock, though for mealing-stones and hammer-stones he used a great variety of material. The use of true quartzite was practically unknown to him.

The most prolific centre of Neolithic culture is in the Ceded Districts, particularly in the neighbourhood of Bellary; notably Peacock Hill, the site of a factory where celts can be found in every stage of manufacture, rough, chipped, or with the rough edges created by the chipping battered into even contours (a condition never found in Palæoliths) or ground and polished. Finished celts are also found in large numbers on the hills of Salem and North Arcot. With Neolithic celts are associated other artifacts in large variety, the commonest being spherical hammer-stones and bun-shaped mealing stones, and crude pottery.

III. The Culture of the Early Iron Age is a doubtful proposition. In the Bellary area evidence of iron-smelting is found in Neolithic sites, but there is no evidence to link this with the relatively advanced art of Tinnevelly (Adichanallūr), Chingleput (Perumbayūr), the Nilgiris, and Hyderabad State (Dornakal, etc.).

The Nilgiri finds (the famous Breeks' collection) are noteworthy for crude animal figures of pottery and bronze bowls of exquisite workmanship.

Perumbayūr is characterized by earthenware sarcophagi which tempt comparison with Babylonia, three-legged vases, stone circles, huge capstones, carved chanks and red-and-black glazed pottery so curiously like that of early Egypt.

Adichanallūr again presents complex artifacts of bronze, to which no parallel can be found, and gold 'diadems' which irresistably suggest Mycenæ.

It would be premature to generalize on the evidence so far unearthed, as it has never yet been critically examined. The absence, however, of any trace of the bull and the frequency of the buffalo, the capstones and stone circles and the complete difference to the methods of disposing of the dead traditional to South India seem sufficient to warrant a date which might fairly be deemed pre-historic.

*Pictographs and Pottery Marks.*—On Peacock Hill, Bellary, are a number of pictographs of men and animals, battered on the weathered surface of the trap rock, which are not improbably contemporaneous with the neolithic settlement. Unfortunately these too have never been published, nor have they been examined by experts in the light of similar rock markings elsewhere.

Lastly, mention must be made of the incised linear markings found on Iron Age pottery, both in the Hyderabad area and in the Madras Presidency. As many as 131 different forms have been recorded, many of them recurring repeatedly in different places, and some of them identical with letters of the undeciphered scripts of the earliest Mediterranean civilizations.

F. J. R.

# A NOTE ON THE ANTHROPOLOGY OF SOUTH INDIA

## I. Geography

CIS-VINDHYAN INDIA presents three main geographical areas: (1) The Deccan Plateau, (2) the Eastern Coastal Plain, and (3) the West Coast.

Across the peninsular south-west, from Madras City to the Palghat Gap in the Western Ghats, runs an area of denudation formed by the Pālār River, the Middle Pennaiyār and the Middle Cauvery, traversed by the Madras-Calicut Railway line, and bounded on the north by the hills that fringe the Southern Deccan, hills tenanted through the ages by dynasties of Border Chieftains or Poligars, many of which still survive. This 'Poligar Belt' is an important factor in South Indian Ethnology.

***Areas of Segregation.***—The above three areas are

areas of 'aggregation' and 'characterization,' in which political, religious and social forces, working on a more or less dense population, have established in each a fairly uniform and distinctive type of culture and social organization. For relics of the earliest strata of society, however, the anthropologist will look to the 'areas of segregation,' of which there are two main groups—

I. The North-East Group: the Agency Tracts, comprising the plateau hinterland of Ganjam, Vizagapatam and Godavari.

II. The Western Group, i.e. the Western Ghats which fall into three divisions—

(1) Southern, the Western Ghats south of the Palghat Gap.

(2) Central, comprising—

(i) the Nilgiris,

(ii) the Wynaad, and

(iii) Coorg.

(3) Northern, comprising the Western Ghats, north of Coorg.

III. The South-East Group, consisting of—

(1) the Nallamalais, and

(2) the hills of Salem, Trichinopoly, North and South Arcot.

## II. Language

To the anthropologist 'South India' spells 'Dravidian,' the name given to a 'family' of languages spoken by nearly sixty-three million people. Yet no genetic connection has yet been established between Dravidian speech and any other tongue spoken outside India.

Out of forty-six Dravidian dialects only four have a literature, but these four languages are spoken by 92 per cent of the total number of Dravidians, and geographical and literary influences have combined to give them a truly national character.

They are—

| | | | |
|---|---|---|---|
| (1) Telugu | ... | 23½ | millions |
| (2) Tamil | ... | 18 | ,, |
| (3) Kanarese | ... | 10½ | ,, |
| (4) Malayalam | ... | 6¾ | ,, |

Telugu and Kanarese prevail northwards of the 'Poligar Belt,' Telugu in the Eastern Deccan and Eastern Coastal Plain, and Kanarese in the Western Deccan, till they merge, the former into Uriya, and the latter into Marāthi. The line between them wavers between the 77° and 78° of latitude.

Tamil is dominant in the Eastern Coastal Plain, south of the Poligar Belt, and laps round the extreme south of the Western Ghats into Travancore, where it loses itself in Malayālam, the language of the West Coast as far north as Kasaragod. North of this Malayālam gives place to Tulu, the language of a cultured people, though it has no literature. Tulu is separated from Konkani by a comparatively modern overflow of Kanarese from the Bednore country on the plateau.

Of the 'uncultured' tongues, four are found on the Nīlgiris (Tōda, Kōta, Kurumba and Badaga), and two in Coorg (Kodagu and Yerava). In the Agency Kandhi (Khond) and Koya prevail, and Dravidian tongues are spoken by the Oraons of the Chota-Nagpur plateau, the Gonds of the Central Provinces, the Malers of the Santal Parganas and the Brahuis of Baluchistan.

The Gadabas and Savars of the Agency Tracts speak languages of the Austric Family, a family which stretches from Madagascar across the Pacific to Easter Island, and from the Punjab to New Zealand.

A word as to script. As a language Telugu stands apart,' all the other Dravidian tongues in South India belonging to the Dravida or Tamilic group. The Kanarese and Telugu alphabets, on the other hand, are adaptations of a Sanskrit prototype, while Tamil and Malayalam scripts possess certain features which cannot be traced to any known origin, and it is certain that the language was reduced to writing before Sanskrit grammarians had anything to do with it. Affinities are surmised between the unknown element in early Tamil script and the undeciphered scripts of the Mediterranean area, but speculation has not yet ripened into proof.

## III. Race

Language, however, is no criterion of race, and the boundaries of race and language rarely coincide. In spite of the paucity of data, three distinct racial strains can be traced in South India.

(*a*) A long headed race (index 72–76), short in stature (1505–1600 mm.), or 'shortish' (1600–1625), with broad (very broad) noses (index 80–95) ;

(*b*) A long headed race (index 72–76), short or shortish in stature (1530-1658 mm.), with a nose of medium breadth (index 71–80) ;

(*c*) A race similar in height and breadth of nose to (*b*) but with a tendency to roundness of head (cephalic index 75–82).

Class (*a*) comprises the jungle tribes of the South (Kādir, Kānikar, Mala Vēdan, Urāli, Shōlaga, Paliyan, Irula, Kurumbar, Paniyan). Some of them (e.g. the Kurumbars of the Nīlgiris) show a tendency to curly hair and negroid features, others do not. It is quite possible that two racial elements are present in them, viz. (*a*) an Australoid strain like the Veddahs of Ceylon, and (*b*) a Negrito strain, derived from an early people akin to the Andamanese. These jungle folk now speak corrupted jargons of the language of the nearest plainsmen. The one thing certain is that they are not 'typical Dravidians,' and 'pre-Dravidian' is the safest term that can be applied to them.

Class (*b*) is the prevailing type of the Tamil and Malayālam areas, and embraces all grades of the population, except for a round-headed element which Mr. J. Hornell has detected among the Parava fishermen of Tinnevelly. The Class (*b*) type extends generally throughout the Telugu and Kanarese country, but in Coorg and in the direction of the Marātha border the round-headed factor, Class (*c*), comes into evidence, an element which is variously attributed to 'Scythians,' the 'Alpine Race' and 'Asiatic Leucoderms'.

Of the tribes and castes examined by Mr. Thurston the highest and lowest tribal or caste averages appearing in each group are tabulated below. It will be noted that the nose gets narrower and the head rounder as the Marātha area is approached.

| Group | Number of tribes or castes sampled | Average nasal index | | Average Cephalic index | | Average stature in cm. | |
|---|---|---|---|---|---|---|---|
| | | MIN. | MAX. | MIN. | MAX | MIN. | MAX. |
| Jungle ... | 9 | 80·1 | 95·1 | 72·9 | 76·4 | 150·5 | 159·8 |
| Malayālam ... | 8 | 71·1 | 81·2 | 72 5 | 76·3 | 153·0 | 165·2 |
| Tamil ... | 17 | 72·4 | 81·5 | 73·0 | 76·2 | 159·7 | 165·8 |
| Telugu ... | 13 | 72·8 | 80·8 | 75·0 | 81·0 | 159·9 | 165·7 |
| Kanarese ... | 22 | 71 2 | 79·4 | 75·6 | 81·7 | 160·8 | 167·2 |
| Tulu ... | 3 | 72·2 | 72·6 | 78·0 | 80·4 | 163·2 | 165·7 |
| Marāthi ... | 4 | 72·2 | 75·8 | 77·8 | 82·2 | 160·3 | 163·4 |
| Orissa [1] ... | 14 | 76·8 | 85·1 | 75·6 | 78·4 | 158·5 | 164·5 |

[1] Risley.

## IV. Social Organization

Socially South India is broken up into a multitude of communities between which marriage is forbidden.

Each community is divided into clans, normally multiple, rarely dual. The system of relationship is 'classificatory,' a system prevailing throughout the Pacific and in North America, a system totally unlike that of the peoples of Aryan and Semitic speech. Under this system one individual bears to another either a 'blood' or 'marital' relationship. Typically the members of a clan are *inter se* 'elder and younger brothers' (*annan-tambi*), and to members of other clans they are 'fathers-in-law and sons-in-law' (*māman-machinan*). My father's brothers are my 'fathers,' their sons are my 'brothers' and their daughters are my 'sisters'. My mother's brothers are my fathers-in-law and their sons are my brothers-in-law and their daughters are my sisters-in-law. 'Cross-cousin marriage' is, of course, the ordinary rule. In some communities it is my mother's brother's daughter, in others my father's sister's daughter, in others either, that must be my bride. Sometimes the rule is optional, but if my mother's brother gives his daughter in marriage without my consent, there will be a row. Sometimes the rule is rigorous, and I have *got* to marry the girl, though she be thirty years of age, and I only six. My father will look after her, and any son she bears to him will be my son. My turn will come only when such 'son' of mine marries. In 'Hinduized' communities, no doubt, the rule is worked more reasonably, but the 'cross-cousin' is always the most suitable bride.

There is, however, another form of marriage, very characteristic of a number of communities, and that is marriage with the daughter of one's elder sister, usually 'clan' sister, sometimes 'own' sister.

Fictitious sonship is not confined to cross-cousin marriage. Leaving aside adoption which is permitted under Brahmanic law, a sonless man may either 'affiliate his son-in-law' (*illatam* as the Telugus call it) or dedicate his daughter as a temple prostitute. In either case, if a son is born, he is grandson and heir to his mother's father. The limit is perhaps reached by the Toda girl, who, though she may conceive a child even by one of her own clansmen, must, in her seventh month, select a man (or even a small boy) from among those with whom her marriage would be permissible to give her the little toy bow and arrow, the gift which is alone recognized as fixing the parentage of the child.

The clan is frequently so far totemistic that the clan name is the name of an animal, plant or inanimate object, and that (more rarely) a *tàbu* is observed by the clansmen in respect to such animal, plant or object. The idea of descent from or kinship with the totem, however, does not exist. In many communities the totem name has given place to the name of an ancestor or ancestral village. This is especially typical of the Telugu clans which are distinguished by their 'house names' (*inti-pĕralu*). The more Hinduized castes adopt or imitate the Brahmanic system of *gōtra*-clans.

Descent and succession are ordinarily in the male line, but Malabar is the classic home of matrilineal succession, coupled with a form of 'hypergamous' marriage contracted and terminable at will (*sambandham*), and associated with polyandry of a non-fraternal type. It is significant that mother-right in Malabar is distinctive of the higher castes and is not found in the lower strata. It cannot, therefore, be called 'aboriginal'. In South Malabar marriage is typically matrilocal, i. e. the husband cannot take his wife to live with him, but must resort to her parent's home.

Vestiges of mother-right are traceable among

Tamils and Telugus, but as a social institution it has vanished at the touch of orthodox Hinduism. In Malabar, however, orthodoxy has undergone a violent change. The Nambūdri Brahmans have abandoned pre-puberty marriage and ensure primogeniture and safeguard their estates by prohibiting the marriage of any but their eldest sons; the younger sons seek solace with Nāyar consorts; and the majority of Nambūdri girls are condemned to perpetual virginity.

Family 'avoidances' have not been closely studied in South India. Her husband's name is *tàbu* to a married woman. The eldest boy, who is usually named after his father's father, is given a nickname to avoid repeating his grandsire's name irreverently. The son-in-law is, as everywhere else, shy of his mother-in-law, but otherwise 'avoidances' do not play a prominent part in social life.

The caste system of South India is merely the expression of the law of endogamy. Many factors combine in India to give this law greater rigour than anywhere else in the world.

First, pride of race, clannishness, the natural reluctance of a man to give his daughter in marriage to a stranger whose standard of living differs from his own, especially if that stranger is his social inferior.

Secondly, there are strong economic reasons for keeping the clan group intact, the interest of real estate, it may be, or the 'trade-union' instinct which holds together those who have a common vocation and enables them to transmit their skill from generation to generation.

Language and religion too come into play. A difference in language almost always, and a difference in religion not seldom, are bars to intermarriage between communities otherwise closely alike.

All these fluid human prejudices have in South India been crystallized by tradition and scripture, and society is a mosaic of infusible tesseræ.

The 'Four Caste' theory of Brahmanic writ does not fit the facts of Dravidian India. Kshattriyas of the classic Rajput type are missing. So also, but for the claims of Telugu Kōmatis, are Vaisyas. Claims to Kshattriya or Vaisya rank are from time to time put forward, but such claims are usually met by ridicule or violence.

The general framework of society in the Tamil, Telugu and Kanarese areas is much the same.

(1) On top are the **Brahmanas**: Vaishnava, Saiva or Madhva, divided among themselves into innumerable endogamous sections, few in numbers but of vast influence.

(2) Then come a multitude of land-owning communities, ranging in status from zamindar to petty ryot. The Telugu Reddi-Kāpus, the Tamil Vellālars, the Kanarese Vakkiligas are ubiquitous within their own areas, and large settlements of the Reddi-Kāpus exist throughout the Tamil country, relics of the ebb and flow of conquest that characterize the 'Unchanging East'. The chieftaincies of the Andhra country are held mostly by Velamas. Typical of the south Chola country are the Kallars (Trichinopoly, Tanjore, Pudukkōttai and North Madura), the Maravas of the Pandya country (Tinnevelly, Ramnad and South Madura), and the Vanniyars (Pallis) of Kongu (Coimbatore and South Salem). Southern Tamilakam is divided among Kallar, Marava and Tōttiya overlords, the last named of Telugu extraction. The Kallars are notable for the use of the boomerang and in some sections for the practice of circumcision.

(3) The trading classes are represented by the so-called Chettis, a vague term covering a number

of interesting communities, mostly Telugu (Kōmati, Bēri, Nagarattu, Nāttukōttai, Janappar, etc.).

(4) The industrial classes comprise—

(*a*) Weavers; Sāles, Togatas and the silk weaving Saurāshtra Brahmans, usually congregated in large numbers in towns, especially in towns which have been the seat of government.

(*b*) Oil-pressers.

(*c*) Toddy-drawers (Nādārs or Shānārs, Idigas, Billavas, Segidis) who bitterly resent the low place assigned them in the social scale by the cultivating castes.

(*d*) The artisans or Visva-Brahmanas (Tamil Kammālan, Telugu Kamsala, Kanarese Pānchāla), a unique guild of five industries—(1) Goldsmiths, (2) Brass-workers, (3) Carpenters, (4) Stone-masons, (5) Blacksmiths—welded into a single community and bitterly antagonistic to other Brahmans.

(*e*) Potters, a community scattered in almost every village and regarded as village servants.

(*f*) Salt workers.

(*g*) Basket-makers, an industry that preserves its 'aboriginal' character.

(5) Herdsmen castes, including the large groups of Telugu Gollas and Tamil Idayas, who pasture cattle, and the Telugu-Kanarese Kurubas, who tend sheep and weave blankets.

(6) Fishermen, of the sea and inland waters, the former the masters of the catamaran and masula-boat, and the latter of the skin-covered coracle.

(7) Menials, the village barber and washerman, and the servants and retainers of *zamindars*.

(8) The serf castes, including the Pallars of the Tamil country and the outcastes, the Paraiyans, Panchamas or Adi-Dravidas of the Tamil, the Sakkiliyas ('Chucklers'), the Mādigas and Mālas of the Telugu country and the Holeyas of Kannada. In addition to these there is a caste of village accountants in North and South Arcot, a caste of temple servants (Sātānis), another of dancing girls, the migratory Oddars who make tanks and wells and quarry stone, a number of thief castes, notably the Koravars who observe *couvade* [1] and like the Kallars

[1] The custom that compels a man to take to bed when his wife is confined.

levy *kāval* fees from the villagers of Salem and other districts for protecting property against theft.

The foreign elements in the population, mainly Marāthis and the nomadic gipsies (Lambādis), acrobats (Dommaras), mendicants and bird-catchers need not be here enumerated. A few aboriginal elements survive in the plains, e.g. the primitive Yānādis near Pulicat Lake.

On the West Coast the social regimentation is of a somewhat different type.

(*a*) In the Malayālam country the sacerdotal hierarchy represented by the Nambūdiri Brahmans, with their sixty-four unorthodox customs and ineffable sanctity, and below them a varied group of 'quasi-Brahman' communities, Ambalavāsis Elayāds, Mussāds, to each of which is traditionally assigned some specific branch of temple worship, or the family priesthood of specific non-Brahman castes.

Then comes a well-marked feudal organization. At the top is the Kshattriya and Sāmantan aristocracy, and below them a many graded congeries of communities grouped under the general name of Nāyars. Some of these communities are of a military type, others are vocational, some of whom (e.g. potters, oil-pressers, coppersmiths, herdsmen) do not pollute by touch and others (e.g. barbers, washermen and weavers) do.

Then come a group of communities which are held to convey 'distance' pollution, the Tiyyans or Izhuvans (clean living people, who, like the Tamil Nādārs, resent the position assigned to them by the Nāyars), the fishermen, (Mukkuvans), artisans, astrologers, herbalists, exorcists and others too numerous to mention.

At the bottom are the servile Cherumans and Pulayans, the Paraiyans, and, lowest of all, the out-caste Nāyādis who pollute a Brahman who comes within 100 feet of them.

An interesting feature of Malayālam society are the 'Paradēsis' or foreigners, who have largely adopted Malayāli customs (the forelock, matrilineal succession, *sambandham*, marriage, etc.). There are the Brahmans of Palghat, the Tulu Embrāntiris, the Konkanis; but perhaps the most notable feature of all is that the most important industrial communities, the weavers and the artisans, together with the traders, are almost all of Tamil origin.

(*b*) Further north in South Kanara the social strata have been disturbed by historical events and the power of chieftains destroyed, but the dominant land-holding communities, the Tulu Bants, for the most part observe matrilineal succession, as do also the Mogēr fishermen.

One other line of social cleavage deserves note, viz. the grouping of certain non-Brahman castes into the Right Hand and Left Hand Factions, a division which is found among Tamil, Telugu and Kanarese alike, and survives among the Chāliyan weavers of Malabar. The origin of these factions has not been satisfactorily explained. Traditionally there are eighteen Right Hand and nine Left Hand castes, but the list differs in different areas. The Paraiyans belong to the Right and the Chucklers to the Left, and it is between these that rows begin. The lead in the Left Hand 'opposition' is taken by the Visva-Brahmana artisans.

The hill tribes belong to a different order. The Khonds, Koyas, Savaras and Gadabas of the Agency Tracts have already been referred to. The Khonds are noted for human sacrifice (meriah), the prototype apparently of 'hookswinging.' On the Ghats of Malabar are the Paniyans who make fire by the sawing' method of Malay. (The fire drill, of various patterns, is the more usual method elsewhere.)

In the Nīlgiris there are the pastoral Tōdas, the agricultural Badagas, the artisan Kōtas, and, on the lower slopes, the jungle Kurumbars. The Wynaad and Coorg present curious mixtures of race and culture which cannot be here unravelled. South of the Palghat Gap are the Vettuvans, whose women-folk wear aprons of leaves, the Kādirs who chip their incisors like the Jakuns of the Malay Peninsula, climb trees like the Dyaks of Borneo and wear combs liked the Negritos of Malacca. In the Nallamalais are the reprobate Chenchus who defy reclamation from crime. The Salem and Arcot Hills are tenanted by a numerous folk, popularly and suggestively called Malayālis, some of whom wear the forelock and the white cotton cloths characteristic of Malabar.

In the Palnis are the Kunnavans and their serfs the Pulaiyans, and further south, the slopes of the Ghats, are haunted by a pitiable remnant of an aboriginal jungle folk, the Paliyans. Unfortunately, except in Dr. Rivers 'Todas,' little intensive scientific investigation has been done on any of the hill tribes, and some of these are fast vanishing under the corrosive influence of civilization.

The 'village community' of South India has been

the subject of much indiscriminate theorizing. There is, of course, the familiar village polity, the headman and accountant, various village servants, the messenger, carpenter, potter, smith, astrologer, barber, washerman and, most interesting of all, the *nīrkatti* who regulates the distribution of water to irrigate the fields of the several ryots with the help of a perforated clepsydra floating in a bowl of water. The village council still survives in some areas and adjudicates in offences against caste proprieties and disputes regarding property. But the elaborate state-recognized village committees of the eleventh and twelfth centuries so vividly depicted in the inscriptions of the Chola Empire have long since vanished. The bedrock of social organization in South India is, however, not the village community but the caste *panchāyat*. In its purest form the unit is the clan hamlet, the men of which are all 'brothers' in the classificatory sense. The several hamlets of a single clan are united in a clan cult, with a recognized cult centre at which the clan festivals are celebrated. Simple disputes within the clan are decided by the clan elders, but appeal against the clan decision and disputes of larger importance lies with the Nād Council, representative of a group of clans, and, in some communities, a higher court exists for a group of Nāds.

This type of polity presents an infinite number of variations. Not infrequently the supreme arbiter is a Brahman Guru, or elsewhere, a high-caste officer, originally appointed by the State. This Nād polity still persists among most of the communities, though sadly disintegrated by our Courts of Law. Typically, the caste council, of whatever grade, is confined to members of the caste, but not infrequently outsiders are associated with it, the village officers it may be, or, as on the Nīlgiris, representatives of all communities within the area.

## V. Religion

Apart from spirit- and ghost-cults (too intricate for discussion here) there are three well-marked religious strata in South India.

(*a*) The Brahmanic cults of Vishnu, Siva, and their consorts, with Vignēsvara, Subrahmanya and, in a less degree, Hanuman, centred mostly in towns.

(*b*) The cult of a consortless Mother Goddess, various in name and aspect, the deity *par excellence* of village life.

(*c*) Serpent worship.

These strata often coalesce, and the Brahmanic cults in particular tend to absorb the other two, adopting the Mother Goddess as a manifestation of Siva's consort, and eliminating the blood sacrifice (particularly buffalo sacrifice) which is part of the normal cult.

The ritual of a Brahmanic temple bears as striking a resemblance to that of ancient Egypt, as the Mother cult of the Mediterranean does to the Amma cults of South India, and the practice of placing the severed foreleg of the victim in the mouth of its decapitated head (as in the buffalo sacrifices of the Telugus and the goat sacrifices of the Nīlgiri Kurumbars) suggests tempting analogies with a well-known rite of ancient Egypt. Pilgrimages are ordinarily associated with a Brahmanic cult. Space forbids enumeration of pilgrim centres. The most noteworthy are Tirupati, Rāmēswaram, Cape Comorin and the five 'lingams of the elements,' Srirangam (water), Kālahasti (wind), Conjeeveram (earth), Tiruvannāmalai (fire) and Chidambaram (ether). The Mahāmakham festival of Kumbakōnam, and the Pushkarams of the Kistna and Godavari Rivers, which occur once in twelve years, attract hundreds of thousands of pilgrims. A similar twelve-year cycle is found in Malabar.

In philosophic Hinduism, South India may justly claim pre-eminence, for, in addition to the Tamil saints, whose traditions are localized mainly in Tanjore District, the three great apostles of Aḍvaita, Visishtadvaita and Dvaita Philosophy (Sankarāchārya, Rāmānujāchārya and Mādhavāchārya) all hail from the South. The spiritual successor of Sri Sankarāchārya is to-day represented by the Jagad-Guru of Sringeri (Kadur District, Mysore State), who shares with the Head of the Kumbakōnam Matha the spiritual supremacy over the Smartha Saivites. Melkōte (Mysore District) still preserves the traditions of Sri Rāmānujāchārya, and Udipi (South Kanara) those of Sri Mādhavāchārya. An interesting factor in South Indian Saivism is the 'Sudra Mathas' of Tanjore District (Dharmapuram, Tiruvāduturai, Tiruppanandāl and Tiruppugalūr).

The Lingāyats or Vīra-Saivas are dissentient Saivites who repudiate Brahman authority. They form a very influential community throughout the Kanarese area. They number about three million. Though they came into being in the twelfth century

A.D. in revolt against Brahmanic caste restrictions, their social organization is now a replica of the caste system. The spiritual needs of the community are provided for by a well-defined ecclesiastical organization of sub-Mathas and branch Mathas, each subordinate to one or other of the five head Mathas of (1) Ujjani (Bellary), (2) Bāle-Honnūr, (3) Sri-Saila (Kurnool), (4) Benares, and (5) Kedarnath (Garhwal, United Provinces). The foundations of Vira Saivism were apparently laid on the ruins of Jainism in the Western Deccan.

Jainism itself, once widespread in South India, is now confined mostly to South Kanara and a group of villages on the borders of the two Arcots.

The Muhammadans are represented by various communities of northern origin which formed the Islamic element in the Deccan Sultanates and are still called Dakkinis; and by the Tamil Labbais and Marakkāyars, the Malayālam Mappilla (Moplahs) and the Telugu Pinjāris. The last named, whose hereditary occupation is cotton cleaning, preserve many Hindu traits.

Christianity and Judaism won a very early foothold on the West Coast, where the Syrian Christians of various rites and Jews 'Black' and 'White still thrive, while legends connecting Saint Thomas with the Mount and Mylapore have lost no vitality by the lapse of centuries.

## VI. Conclusion

The anthropology of South India presents a bewildering variety of problems, the investigation of which has hardly yet begun. Cultural affinities with the Dravidian-speaking peoples can be traced in every continent and clime except perhaps the Arctic Circle. The evidence of the oldest strata points eastwards, to Indonesia, Australia, the Pacific and America, but the main body of custom, especially religion, is far more suggestive of the Mediterranean. But origins are evasive things, and all cultures are complex. Whatever its affinities may be, the culture of the Dravidian peoples is their own and its origin is Indian.

F. J. R.

# SOME PROBLEMS OF MARINE ZOOLOGY IN SOUTH INDIA

APART from the fishes and to some extent the larger crustaceans and echinoderms, the marine fauna of South India has received little attention. The only list attempting to give a synopsis of the general fauna of any one locality is that first published in 1890 by Mr. E. A. Thurston, then Superintendent of the Madras Museum, and subsequently re-issued in a revised form in 1895 as Museum Bulletin No. 3. This deals principally with the fauna of Rameswaram Island and the shallow waters of the western coastline of the Gulf of Mannar. The eastern section of the same area in 1903–6 received fuller and more exhaustive treatment in the series of five fine volumes of *Ceylon Pearl Fishery Reports* issued by the Royal Society under the editorship of Professor Herdman, F.R.S. This latter region though politically belonging to Ceylon must be classed as pertaining faunistically to the same zoogeographical area as that treated of by Thurston; the two lists are complimental and must be read together. The main outlines of the fauna of the Gulf of Mannar have been drawn; it now remains for details to be filled in, the nomenclature of the lists brought up to date and correlated, and the accuracy of the diagnoses verified. For no other portion of the coast do any lists exist and this is an investigation worthy of early attention by the Zoological Survey of India when an enlarged staff becomes available. Local marine faunas on the Madras coasts fall into tour sections—(*a*) The Malabar Coast, (*b*) The Gulf of Mannar, (*c*) Palk Bay, and (*d*) The Coromandel Coast. The two former have always been continuous at their southern ends, but there was undoubtedly a land barrier dividing these from the second set of two in recent geological time along the line of islands and sandbanks now stretching between India and Ceylon at the head of the Gulf of Mannar. This land connection in turn was preceded by a time when Ceylon was of considerably smaller dimensions than at present, when no islands dotted the sea between Ceylon and India and when the south-eastern margin of India was much further to the west than it now is. Under such conditions the wide sea that separated India and Ceylon in those days permitted of unrestricted faunistic intercourse between what are now the Gulf of Mannar and the Coromandel sea. At no far distant epoch there must have been greater faunistic uniformity in the Madras marine area than to-day, and many of the differences we find in closely allied species on the West and East Coasts may, in all probability, be dated as having arisen subsequent to the uplift of land that placed an impassable barrier between the sedentary and semi-sedentary forms without pelagic larvæ living on opposite sides of the once continuous Adam's Bridge. It is for this reason that an intensive comparative study of the faunas of the Gulf of Mannar and of Palk Bay and the Coromandel Coast is particularly desirable, for knowledge of the geological fact of the recent land connection of Ceylon with India enables us to date the origin of differences between those forms that differ varietally in the two areas. This valuable line of research into the recent evolution of varieties and species is applicable more especially to those molluscs whereof the young pass their larval stages within capsules anchored in the sand or attached to shells or stones. So far the Indian conch (*Turbinella pirum*, L.) has alone been studied in this manner. The result showed that distinct varieties occur in the two areas, with a marked fan-outlined overflow of the southern variety through the main channels between the islands and sandbanks dividing the two regions.[1] The local representatives of the families of the Rachiglossa, which include the Muricidæ, Fasciolariidæ, Doliidæ, Volutidæ, and Buccinidæ, having analogous larval history to the Turbinellidæ, are the most likely to exhibit parallel differences, whereof the study may throw light upon the factors governing the evolution of new forms, whether by mutation, adaptation to local conditions though natural selection, or otherwise. An interesting point in this study is the fact that a mutation of the Indian conch resulting in the production of shells with reversed whorls (sinistral forms), showed a tendency to become fixed during recent years in the south-west of Palk Bay, where a fishery for this shell is carried on. Year after year shells of the new form were found; in one year as many as twelve. Such shells are very

[1] Hornell, J.—'The Indian Varieties and Races of the Genus Turbinella.' *Mem. Ind. Mus.*, Vol. VI, 1916, pp. 111-122.

valuable and as a consequence the divers sought specially for them and appear now to have killed off the family so characterized as none has been found for two years past.

Among other lines of promising investigation for which the fauna of Madras waters affords special opportunities may be mentioned the following:— Commensalism, parasiticism, masking and other protective devices, aberrant habits, the adaptation of sea forms to a life in freshwater, the causes of fish migrations and, widest field of all, study of the larval histories of all these animals, a practically untouched field awaiting the patient harvester.

Commensalism is particularly common in the Indian marine fauna. At Madras, in the debris from fishermen's nets, we often find the little crab *Dorippe dorsipes* holding over its back a valve of Tellina on which is seated a pale-coloured anemone. In Palk Bay a spider-crab similarly secures protection by trimming (and concealing) its carapace, beset with stiff recurved bristles, with numbers of the pretty black and white striped *Synapta striata*, distasteful to other creatures by reason of the myriads of tiny calcareous anchors embedded in the skin. The anemone *Adamsia*, as in Europe, is found frequently in partnership with one of the larger Pagurids. The velvet-clothed *Dromia* is another common crab that exhibits great sagacity in utilizing the services of another animal for masking. Usually it breaks off a fragment of a sponge or of a compound ascidian and holds it over its back by means of its posterior legs till in the course of time it forms a complete mantle, fitted exactly to the shape of the crab and hiding it completely. Another species has modified this habit and lives rather as a parasite within the Alcyonarian *Spongodes*, excavating a tunnel within the thick stalk of its host, open at each end. Perhaps the most curious of partnerships is the association of the Gephyrean worm (*Aspidosiphon*) with the little cup-corals *Heteropsammia* and *Heterocyathus*, quite common on pebbly bottom in the Gulf of Mannar. But it is impossible to mention even a tithe of the common Madras commensals; suffice it to draw attention to the wide range of this habit. The majority have a cœlenterate involved in the partnership: crabs, alphæids, little cypræids, and ophiurids live with sponges and gorgonids; amphipods and fishes with medusæ; pea-crabs with bivalves and holothurians; aviculids with gorgonids and zoophytes; polychæt worms and lamellibranchs lodge with certain sponges, and give assistance to their hosts by stiffening and strengthening the tissues.

Where commensalism ends and parasiticism begins is often difficult to say. Comparatively little marine work has been done in the latter subject in India, what little having been restricted to certain groups of fishes (Elasmobranchs and the Balistidæ) and to a few lamellibranchs (*Meleagrina margaritifera* and *Placuna placenta*). Even here the work done is not nearly exhaustive and little is known of the internal anatomy of the forms already described. These consist principally of cestodes, trematodes, and copepoda. In practically no case has the life-history been satisfactorily worked out; everything yet remains to be done in correlating the larval forms of the parasitic worms found profusely in many molluscs and crustaceans with the sexual stages present in fishes. Under exceptional circumstances these larvæ induce the formation of pearls in numerous species of molluscs, but with the exception of the pearl oyster and Placuna, no work has been attempted in this promising field. I would direct attention specially to the pearls produced sometimes in profusion by the freshwater mussels (*Unionidæ*) and in the common green-mussel of our backwaters (*Mytilus viridis*); Surada reservoir and Sonapur backwater, both in Ganjam District, are the best localities for the investigation of these two problems.

Study of colouration and of the wonderfully varied means whereby marine animals seek to obtain some measure of immunity from the attacks of their enemies, or such camouflage as will enable them to surprise their prey, is another subject that will well repay attention in our seas. The kaleidoscopic conditions that prevail on the bottom provide infinite variety in environment, with the result that a high premium is set upon successful adaptative devices. It may be camouflage by the adoption of bright and seemingly conspicuous colouring but so broken up that it disappears from view much more quickly than if self-coloured in some neutral tint, as seen in many of the brilliantly coloured coral fishes (*Chætodons*), or it may be the converse, perfect approximation to the colour and even the form of the environment, as seen in the colouring of the upper side of certain soles, simulating the sand where they live, the reddish frills and furbelows of the scorpion-fishes (*Pterois* spp.) or the striped brown and white shells of ***Avicula zebra*** that lives among the pinnules of one of the giant Plumularian zoophytes (***Halicornaria insignis***). In a desultory way a considerable number of observations have been recorded, but most are essentially superficial and not based on careful study; they all require re-investigation. Quite a number of instances of vivid colouring exist, difficult or almost impossible to explain in our present limited understanding of these things—some may be of the nature of warning colours as is the orange and black of the sea-snake (*Hydrophis spiralis*), but this explanation fails in the case of the big Holothurian (***Cucumaria tricolor***) striped alternately pale purple and canary yellow. Possibly the latter is a mere expression of the tint values of certain excretory waste products—uric acid in some colour combination.

The boring and burrowing habits of many marine animals have often great economic importance, because of the damage they inflict upon wood-work immersed in the sea — ships' bottoms, the piles of piers and jetties and the like. The ship-worms (***Teredo*** spp.) are the worst of these and are peculiarly active and dangerous in the warm Indian seas. More work on the local species is needed, as also on the species and habits of the rock-burrowing molluscs (*Lithodomus, Tridacna* and others) which excavate homes in coral blocks, and of the Pholadidæ, which in these seas prefer clays and floating wood rather than rock. The burrowing Echinid (*Echinostrephus molare*) is another rock excavator of considerable importance in the neighbourhood of coral reefs, helping to disintegrate dead reef coral, while certain isopods play the same part in regard to wooden piling, often completing the destruction begun by Teredo. Another destructive influence of much economic importance is that of the boring sponges, Clionidæ, of which there are several species. Shells honeycombed with the tunnels of these sponges are termed 'wormed' in the trade circles that deal with pearl-shell, conchs and edible oysters.

The sand-burrowing habits of many species of molluscs also call for investigation, while the means by which the sea-pens can sink rapidly into partial concealment in the sand is notable. The habits of the gregarious sand-burrowing anemone (*Sphenopus*) are also little known.

Madras by reason of the great brackish estuarine lagoons or backwaters that stretch parallel along the coast for hundreds of miles provides a rich field for the study of the acquisition of tolerance, more or less complete, of freshwater conditions by various marine organisms. Naturally fishes are the most obvious and useful for study, as those marine or estuarine fishes that are readily adaptable to acclimatization in freshwater may prove of value to the inland pisciculturist. In Madras the enquiries of the Fisheries Department have already resulted in the utilization of two such species, viz. *Etroplus suratensis* and one of the Mullets (*Mugil troscheli*). The former is now being regularly used for stocking purely freshwater tanks in the very heart of the country: in these it breeds as freely as in brackish backwaters. The second does not breed in inland tanks, but owing to its tolerance of freshwater in the fingerling stage, and the rapidity of its growth, it is valuable for stocking tanks which hold water only for eight months in a year. The acclimatization of some of the smaller crustacea of our estuaries to freshwater conditions is another line of experiment and enquiry of much potential value, for many inland streams lack enough of such food to sustain any large fish population, which as a consequence tend to become stunted in size and fewer in number than would otherwise be the case.

The specialized fauna of purely muddy areas is another subject of enquiry that can readily be pursued on the Madras coast. Such areas are found off and in the deltas of the Kistna and Godavari, in Palk Bay and Strait below the six-fathom line, and nearly everywhere along the west coast, close inshore. Very peculiar local mud banks are also found here and there along the west coast; their origin has been the subject of various theories, but much more work requires to be done before any of these can be accepted; so far as I know, no investigation of their fauna and flora has ever been attempted. Were this to be done, probably it would shed light on the origin of these peculiar accumulations of soft light mud. Among the habitues of ordinary muddy bottom the best examples known at present are a polynoid polychæt (*Panthalis melanonotus*), fairly common in Palk Bay, that forms gelatinous tubular dwellings in the mud, the windowpane oyster (*Placuna placenta*), thin and plate-shaped, used for glazing purposes in Portuguese India and in China, and a certain number of gastropods.

Last and most important of all problems awaiting workers is the investigation of the development of all these animals; our knowledge of this subject is slight and wholly fragmentary. To take special problems of economic importance alone, we have absolutely no knowledge of the life-histories of the oil sardine (*Sardinella longiceps*) and the mackerel (*Scomber microlepidotus*), which furnish in the aggregate a greater total weight to our fishermen than all other kinds of fish together. We know nothing definitely, though we may theorize plausibly, on the causes that bring them to certain sections of our coast in immense myriads in normal years or the reasons for their dearth in others; we have no knowledge of their breeding habits, where they go when they desert our inshore waters, and a dozen other points of vital importance to our fishing industries. As is the case off the coast of North America, it may be that the apparent dearth of mackerel is merely due to the schools in certain years being further to sea than in normal years and so beyond the knowledge and fishing ability of our fishermen. All these problems await solution and those who make contribution will be notable contributors to the country's prosperity. The problem of the location of the breeding grounds of the Indian eels (*Anguilla* spp.) is another of great interest of which we have absolutely no knowledge at present.

J. H.

# THE GEOLOGICAL STRUCTURE OF THE MADRAS PRESIDENCY

AFTER C. S MIDDLEMISS, ESQ., C.I.E., M.A., F.R.S.[1]

THE Madras Presidency consists geologically of an area of Archæan gneisses and schists, and ancient plutonic rocks, on which are superimposed the isolated basin of younger Pre-cambrian (Purana) sediments forming the Kadapah and Karnul area, and the south-eastern extremity of the Lower Gondwana formation of the Godavari basin, and along the eastern coast a broken belt of Upper Gondwana and Cretaceous rocks, while near Rajahmundry is a small isolated outcrop of basaltic lava flows of Deccan Trap age. Along both the east and west coasts of the Presidency, and fringing the above described platform of ancient Archæan rocks with its superimposed sediments is a coastal belt of Younger Tertiary and recent coastal deposits.

[1] Compiled from the article in the *Imperial Gazetteer of India*, Madras, I, with minor additions and modifications in view of recent research and discoveries.

*Archæan Rocks.*—The Archæan group of ancietn crystalline and metamorphic rocks is one that remained practically undifferentiated for a long time Two distinct landmarks in the advance of our knowledge stand out prominently in comparatively recent years: namely, the recognition and mapping over large areas by Mr. R. Bruce Foote of, what he regarded as, a younger sub-group, the Dharwars of Southern India; and Sir Thomas H. Holland's discovery of the charnockite family of genetically related Archæan plutonic intrusive rocks. The Dharwar rocks recognized by Foote were those which he described generally as 'sub-metamorphic'. He regarded them as resting unconformably on the granitoid gneisses, and as being younger generally than the rest of the crystalline complex. The bands of Dharwars exposed in South India were regarded as mere remnants of a great spread of the system of rocks which once covered the gneisses. The rocks of the system include — hornblendic and chloritic schists, hæmatitic quartzites, phyllites and sometimes metamorphosed conglomerates. The hornblende-schists are sometimes altered basic igneous rocks which occasionally retain the original doleritic structure. The whole assemblage of rocks thus resembles generally those known as the Lower Huronian of Canada, and the various occurrences of the kind associated with the Archæan basement complex in different parts of the world. Some of the gneissose granites show locally an intrusive trespass with regard to the Dharwars; in other cases pebbles of gneiss are found in the conglomerates of the Dharwars. It thus appears that some of the gneissose granites are younger, and some much older, than the typical Dharwars. But there is a marked contrast between the age of the Dharwars and associated gneisses and schists, and the unmetamorphosed Kadapahs and other sedimentary rocks resting on them; hence the various kinds of gneisses and schists have been grouped with the Dharwar types to form the Archæan group (T. H. Holland, *Imperial Gazetteer* I, p. 59, 1907). This arrangement differs from that recognized by R. Bruce Foote. The Mysore Geological Department, however, in their work on the Dharwars, have come to the conclusion that as a whole they are older than the gneissic complex with which they are associated. The Dharwars have been split into two divisions, hornblende schists and epi-diorites (altered lava flows) below, with chlorite schists above. The gneiss is considered to be intrusive into both of these, and the intrusion took place by a series of lateral invasions of more or less horizontal sills of varying dimensions, and different in character from the ordinary intrusion of an acid igneous rock. The so-called 'conglomerates' at the base of the hornblende schists in the Kolar belt, and at various horizons above in other areas, are looked on as autoclastic crush formations.

For the purposes of this handbook, however, the Archæans of the Madras Presidency may be divided into three groups, the interrelationships of which may best be left undefined: The Dharwars; thin-bedded schistose gneiss; and massive ortho-gneisses. The massive ortho-gneisses are particularly prominent in the flat elevated plains of Coimbatore and the middle and southern parts of Salem, in the south of Malabar and Bellary, and in the western parts of the Vizagapatam Agency tracts, Ganjam, and Nellore. Monazite is a valuable economic mineral derived from the Archæan rocks of Madras. It is found chiefly in Travancore and Cochin, and its home seems to be in the ortho-gneisses of that area.

The thin-bedded schistose gneiss is less homogeneous than the foregoing group. It contains much mineral wealth. It is sparsely dotted about in Salem and Coimbatore, where it includes crystalline marble and iron ores. Probably also the enormous iron ore deposits of Kanjamalai, the Javadi Hills, and other localities belong to it. These have been worked from time immemorial, and were once smelted by the Porto Novo Iron Company.

The lowest and richest band at the foot of Kanjamalai is seventy feet thick, but only yields an average of less than 40 per cent of iron, thus putting it out of the scope of successful modern commercial exploitation.

The Dharwars have an extensive development in Mysore, and are also to be traced through Bellary, Anantapur, Cudappah, and the extreme northern parts of Salem, and possibly in the Wynaad and in Coimbatore.

From the economic point of view the most important section of the Archæan group is the Dharwar system in which the principal metalliferous deposits are found, including those of iron, manganese and gold, bedded hematitic ores of great richness in their lower parts being especially abundant in the Native State of Sandur, while all the chief gold-bearing reefs that have yet been discovered in Southern India, including the important Kolar Gold Fields in Mysore, occur in Dharwar rocks.

The Archæan plutonic rocks are distinguished from the three sub-groups already described by possessing more uniformity of structure over large areas, and a mineral composition resembling that of known igneous rocks. Hence they are considered to be consolidated relics of what were once fused magmas. The best known of them is Sir Thomas Holland's charnockite series. Besides its first described locality at Saint Thomas's Mount near Madras, this appears in the well-marked, rugged masses of the Nilgiris, Shevaroys, and Palnis, and occurs as bands in Coimbatore, Salem, and Vizagapatam, as well as in Ganjam, South Arcot, and the Wynaad. In the neighbourhood of Palakod in Salem it carries corundum crystals formed as a contact mineral. Test excavations yielded 78½ lbs. of corundum to the ton of matrix. In the upland *taluks* of Salem a very different and characteristic biotite gneissose granite builds moderately elevated plateaux surmounted by cones and *drugs*. The same variety is met with in the Wynaad, Bellary, Vizagapatam, and North and South Arcot, where it is frequently coarsely porphyritic, forming bold and picturesque domes of rock.

In the Eastern Ghats and neighbouring coastal tracts, however, the Archæan formations differ considerably in general facies from the Archæan rocks in the portions of the Presidency already referred to, the most striking difference lying in the general and widespread occurrence of garnet in the rocks of the Eastern Ghats as contrasted with its purely local occurrence elsewhere; khondalite (graphite-garnet-sillimanite-quartz-schist) and garnet gneisses taking the place of the Dharwar schists and normal ortho-gneisses, whilst the rocks of the charnockite series are also generally garnetiferous in this area.

*Eparchæan Interval.*—After the formation of these three Archæan sub-groups and their modification and metamorphism by reason of the plutonic magmas just considered, a vast interval of time appears to have ensued, during which all the rock stages hitherto formed suffered a final compression into closely packed folds, with upheaval and erosion by atmospheric agencies into great table-lands or denudation planes, before being once more depressed below the ocean to receive as sediments the still very ancient Purana group which comes next above them.

About the end of the Eparchæan interval, or during the early parts of the Kadapah epoch, come a number of younger intrusive igneous rocks. Among the pegmatites in these, especially in Nellore, good mica for economic purposes is found. Rare earth mineral, such as samarskite and columbite also occur as accessories. Other pegmatites have yielded aquamarine crystals in times past (as at Pattalai in Coimbatore), as well as fine quartz crystals and amethyst; and yet others near Sivamalai in Coimbatore have developed corundum crystals in considerable quantity, which have been dug and used by lapidaries.

Dykes of various descriptions are a very common feature over large areas of Central and Eastern Madras—especially in the Deccan districts, North Arcot, and Salem, where they sometimes form marked features across the plains. There are several examples of dunite or chromite-olivine rock, the principal of which forms a great mass in the Chalk Hills near Salem, where chromite mines have been worked and magnesite is still being quarried.

*The Purana Group.*—The Purana Group of

apparently azoic sedimentary rocks includes in Madras what are known as the Kadapah and Karnul series. These are typically developed in the districts of the same names, where they form a great crescent-shaped outlier or completely isolated basin, 200 miles long by 100 miles wide in its widest part. Their much more gently inclined strata give to the country an array of parallel scarps, ridges, and flat-topped plateau-like hills, averaging 1,750 feet in elevation, which easily mark it off from the surrounding lowlands and rugged uplands of Archæan rocks.

The lower series, the Kadapahs, are more than ten-times as thick as the overlying Karnuls. The latter series embraces within the moderate thickness of 1,200 feet four stages in conformable descending order. The last and lowest of these, the Banganapalle stage, is a sandstone with grits and pebble beds composed of clay, quartzite chert, and jasper pebbles, and diamonds have been found here by the local inhabitants, who have carried considerable workings into the rock and also among the distributed surface gravels derived from them. The diamonds are octahedra with curved facets, and from their freshness it is considered that although they cannot be inherent in the rock, they cannot have been carried far as pebbles from their original source, which is considered by some to be igneous effusions of upper Kadapah (Bijawar) age.

*Lower Gondwanas.*—The succeeding rock system, the first in the Presidency that is fossiliferous, begins with a formation, the Gondwana, which is a characteristically Indian freshwater deposit with plant remains and coal-beds. Only the southeastern extremity of one shallow trough of the Lower Gondwanas stretches into the Madras Presidency. This outcrop occurs on the left bank of the Godavari river between thirty and forty miles west-north-west of Rajahmundry. It includes five square miles near Bedadanol of coarse, pale, felspathic sandstones with carbonaceous shale seams, and a few similar patches along the Godavari, partly in the Nizam's Dominions and partly in British territory. The value of the coal-fields here has long been an important question, since they constitute the only known possible source of that mineral in Madras. The Bedadanol field was originally tested by Dr. W. King, who reported unfavourably on it ; but there has recently been a revival of interest in the field, and the Government of Madras are at present undertaking a series of test bore-holes across the field, situated at sites selected by Mr. Harold Walker in 1919, in order to decide definitely whether workable seams of coal occur or not.

*Upper Gondwanas.*—The Upper Gondwanas are represented only by a broken belt of outliers, fifteen miles broad in their widest part, along the east coast of the Presidency. The series comprises a three-fold division, from 200 to 300 feet thick, of sandstones above and below, with shales between. In some of the sandstones plant fossils have been found, and in the shales marine fossils—among them ammonites.

*Cretaceous Beds.*—In Trichinopoly District the narrow strip of Upper Gondwanas is overlain on the east by the cretaceous beds of the area. They are very richly fossiliferous, and have yielded altogether about 800 species, of which a large proportion are cephalopods and gasteropods.

*Deccan Trap.*—Near Rajahmundry an isolated, interrupted narrow band of volcanic rocks, of the usual Deccan Trap character, occurs on both banks of the Godavari. It extends for about thirty-five miles from east-north-east to west-south-west. On the left bank of the Godavari the Trap is resting on metamorphic rocks wherever the lower beds are seen, while on the right bank it is resting on Upper Gondwana rocks. The whole thickness of the volcanic series in this area nowhere appears to exceed about 200 feet, and in places is not more than 100 feet. The exposure is about 210 miles distant from the nearest point of the great Deccan Trap area.

*Cuddalore Sandstone.*—Along the east coast, from Rajahmundry to Tinnevelly District, there is a peculiar formation consisting of soft standstones and grits, which forms a low slope dipping at a very slight angle towards the sea. It contains silicified wood in large quantity. Similar beds, the Warkalli beds, are found on the west coast near Quilon in analogous positions. The geological age of these beds is probably Later Tertiary.

*Laterite.*—Both High-level Laterite and Low-level Laterite occur in the Madras Presidency. The low-level variety is found along all the coast regions, while the high-level variety is found on some of the higher plateaux inland—where it is about eighty feet thick—especially in the neighbourhood of Bellary and Kadapah, and in the Vizagapatam Agency. Laterite hardens on exposure and makes a useful building stone.

*Cave Deposits.*—The Billa Surgam cave deposits in Kurnool District are encrusted with stalagmite. They consist of red marl full of mammalian bones, five of the species represented being now extinct, while some of the living forms are African species.

*Recent Deposits.*—The recent deposits of Madras include the older alluvium of the larger rivers, such as the Godavari, Kistna, Cauvery, etc.; the coast and deltaic alluvium, from 50 to 500 feet thick; and all the younger alluvium of the present river-beds, the mud banks of the coasts, and the peat deposits on plateaux such as the Nilgiris. At Pondicherry this formation has yielded an artesian water-supply. In Tinnevelly District evidence of recent subsidence is furnished by a submerged forest.

M. S.

# BIOLOGICAL WORK IN MADRAS

THE Madras Presidency was the scene of the earliest biological work done in India, both as regards Botany and Zoology. In 1674 Henry van Rheede, Governor of Dutch Malabar, had specimens of the plants of his province collected and sent to Cochin, where they were drawn and described in Malayalam. From Malayalam the descriptions were translated through Portuguese into Latin. The resultant work was sent to Europe and published in Amsterdam in 1686–1703 under the title of 'Hortus Malabaricus'.

No attempt to follow up this work appears to have been made till 1768, when John Koenig, a former pupil of Linnæus, came to Tranquebar as Physician and Naturalist to the Danish Missionary Settlement in the Carnatic. His enthusiasm resulted in the formation of the botanical 'Society of United Brothers,' and led him to obtain a post as Naturalist to the Nawab of Arcot and in 1778 to the East India Company.

In 1782 Patrick Russell, the first Indian Zoologist, landed at Vizagapatam, where he spent about seven years. He became deeply interested in Koenig's botanical work, and on the death of latter in 1785 succeeded him as Naturalist to the East India Company. In 1789 he returned to England, where he prepared for publication Koenig's work, as well as his own accounts of 'Coromandel Serpents' and 'Coromandel Fishes'. He was succeeded by William Roxburgh, who had arrived in Madras as Assistant Surgeon in 1776 and was transferred to Bengal in 1793. Roxburgh's main botanical work was on the flora of the Coromandel, and he published on this a very fine series of coloured plates which are still unsurpassed for accuracy and beauty. His *Flora Indica*, though dealing with the flora of the whole country, was founded on his knowledge of the plants of this Presidency, supplemented with that gained as Curator of the Botanic Gardens in Calcutta.

Robert Wight, the author of the earliest English books on Indian Botany, as well as of numerous papers, joined the East India Company's service at Madras as Assistant Surgeon in 1819, succeeded Shuter as Naturalist to the Company in Madras in

1826, holding this post, however, for only two years, it being abolished in 1828. In 1836 he was appointed Superintendent of Cotton Cultivation and of the Experimental Cotton Farm at Coimbatore, retiring in 1853. He was the greatest of South Indian botanists. His great work of seven thick quarto volumes of plates is the standard work of reference of its kind to-day; but it was not merely a collection of drawings, much critical work was put into it. Two other quarto books in which some of these plates were reproduced were *Spicilegium Neilgherrense* and illustrations of Indian Botany. He also published papers on new species and genera in the journal of the Madras Literary Society, in his contributions to the flora of British India, and with Arnott in the *Prodromus Floræ Peninsulæ Indiæ Orientalis*.

T. C. Jerdon joined the Madras Medical Service in 1835, and between then and 1852, when he was transferred to Bengal, laid the foundations which enabled him to obtain facilities for his subsequent epoch-making works on the Birds and Mammals of India as a whole. Similarly, Francis Day, who joined the same service in 1852, laid the foundations of his work on Indian Fishes in this Presidency.

But in spite of the work of these zoological pioneers, the fauna of Madras city and its immediate neighbourhood has as yet been very little studied, largely, no doubt, on account of the much greater richness and varied interest of the Malabar Zone, with its slight but curiously definite African affinities, and of the Nilgiri and other hill ranges. This is the more to be regretted in view of the efforts being made to interest local schools in nature study—especially as marine, estuarine, and freshwater conditions are all represented, as well as somewhat varied terrestrial conditions including sand-dunes and salt-marshes.

The last of the pre-modern botanists was Colonel Beddome. His chief collecting ground was the hilly tracts of Tinnevelly, a region since his day neglected. But as Conservator of Forests he gained an immense knowledge of the trees of the Presidency, and published two large folio works of illustrations and descriptions. He also wrote what is still the standard work on the ferns of India, and published a quarto volume of plates of the ferns of South India, as well as various smaller papers published at intervals from 1863 to 1883. Other collectors of note were Lawson and Leschenault, the former contributing afterwards part of the first volume of Hooker's *Flora of India*.

With the publication of this great work, of which Hooker expressed the hope in his preface that it would be the basis of further and more intensive study of the floras of the different parts of the country, botanical activity in this direction on the contrary died down. In spite of sporadic collections, by the Government Botanist and amateurs, practically no critical work was done and none at all published till the beginning of the second decade of this century. This was in part due, at any rate towards the close of the last century, to the rise in the estimated importance of applied botany, which, with the reorganization of the Agricultural Department, held the field and, with the many important problems awaiting solution, compelled attention.

F. G. H. AND P. F. F.

## THE AGRICULTURAL COLLEGE AND RESEARCH INSTITUTE, COIMBATORE

THE Agricultural College and Research Institute is situated three miles from the town of Coimbatore and about twenty-five miles from the foot of the Nilgiris. It is reached from Madras by one night's journey on the Mettupalaiyam mail train.

The institution comprises a Teaching College and Research Institute, with the necessary quarters for staff, hostel, playing grounds, etc., the Central Farm and two Plant Breeding Stations, the total area occupied being little short of 600 acres.

### TEACHING COLLEGE

This is at present housed with the Research Institute in one main building containing a number of well-fitted laboratories and lecture-rooms. A separate building is, however, under construction, for teaching purposes only, with increased accommodation. The present number of students in residence is 118.

There are two courses of instruction :—

(1) A two-year course in which a thorough training is given in practical agriculture, with as much science as is necessary, but with no lectures on science subjects as such. This course leads to the Proficiency Certificate.

(2) A three-year, post-Intermediate, course in agriculture and the related sciences. Here the science subjects are taught as such, but specially in their relation to agriculture. Negotiations are in progress for the affiliation of the College with the Madras University, and when this has been brought about, the degree of B.Sc. (Agriculture) will be substituted for the Diploma in Agriculture, that is now awarded to students of this course.

*Central Farm.*—The farm possesses an area of 280 acres of cultivable land. It is mainly used for instructional purposes, though some experimental work also is undertaken. A wide range of soils is represented, including dry land, both black and red soils, garden land and wet land. All the principal crops of the Presidency are grown, and the students thus obtain practical experience in all the main types of cultivation. Attached to the farm are an up-to-date dairy, a veterinary hospital and shops for carpentry and blacksmithy.

## RESEARCH INSTITUTE

Investigations in the chief branches of science connected with agriculture are carried out by a number of scientific officers. Some of these are engaged entirely on research work; others are also partly engaged in teaching.

The experimental work varies considerably, from research on scientific matters of fundamental importance to a study of the practical application of known scientific facts. In addition there is a certain amount of routine work, such as chemical analyses, seed-germination tests, examination of material sent in for report on insect and fungoid pests, etc.

The following is a brief summary of the chief lines of work of the various sections.

*Cotton Specialist.*—This section was started in 1920 and land is now being acquired for a Cotton Breeding Station. The work is restricted almost entirely to Cambodia cotton on the following lines:—

(1) Isolation in pure culture of different types of Cambodia.

(2) Similar isolation of types from Cambodia × Bourbon.

The objects aimed at are the production of—(*a*) a type of Cambodia giving a heavy yield per acre of lint averaging 25 mm. in length, (*b*) a type with the drought-resisting qualities of Bourbon combined with the heavy—yielding qualities of Cambodia.

In addition crosses have been made between a long-linted good quality Indicum and a short-linted high-yielding Roseum, the object being to combine the large seed and boll, weight of lint per seed and earliness of Roseum, with the length and strength of lint of the Indicum type.

The technique of examination of the various characters is being studied. A method of measuring lint length, and the relation between combed length and single-fibre length have been worked out.

*Economic Botanist.*—Plant-breeding work on rice occupies practically the whole time of this section. The field work is carried out on the Paddy Breeding Station, which occupies about thirty acres. Improved strains are being raised by single-plant selections from important varieties, and also by crossing good varieties with a view to combining the good qualities of both parents. These strains are tested in the field by means of a system of plots for which the experimental error has been accurately determined.

A study is in progress of the method of inheritance of varietal characters. About thirty Mendelian factors have been worked out and numerous cases of *linkage* determined. An attempt is being made to analyse some of the characters of most direct economic value and to determine the factors responsibl A special study of linkage is being made with a view to tracing any connections there may be between such economic characters and the many simple characters already worked out.

*Entomologist.*—The present research work is confined almost entirely to a study of various pests. An Insectary is attached to the section, for the study of habits and life-histories, with a compound in which the crops concerned are grown.

Full life-histories are being worked out for the Pink Boll Worm (*Platyedra gossypiella*), Saunders, and the Cotton Stem Weevil (*Pempheres affinis*). Their seasonal occurrence and the amount of damage done by each is being studied, and figures are being collected to test the effect of the enforcement of the Pest Act. Other points receiving attention are the possibility of abnormal boll fall caused by infection of young bolls by bacteria, through insect agency, and the control and bionomics of ***Schehobius incertellus*** (bipunctifer). Systematic work is in progress on the Coccidæ and parasitic Hymenoptera. Notes bearing on Medical Entomology are made as opportunity occurs.

*Agricultural Bacteriologist*.—The following work is being carried out in this section :—

(1) Bacterial diseases of cotton.

(2) Nitrogen fixation in soils of different types during different seasons.

(3) Biological analysis of South Indian soils (dry land, garden land and wet land).

(4) Determination of the value of ammonium sulphate as a manure for cotton.

*Agricultural Chemist*.—The investigations on hand include the following subjects :—

(*a*) The availability of the phosphatic nodules of Trichinopoly for paddy, and action of different composts.

(*b*) The action of calcium cyanamide on Madras soils.

(*c*) The estimation of active nitrogen resulting

from the decomposition of oil cakes in different kinds of soils.

(*d*) The manurial requirements of the coconut and cotton plants.

(*e*) The malting of cholam.

(*f*) Improvement in the making of coconut jaggery.

(*g*) Standardization of methods of analysis.

In addition to Laboratory work, investigations are duplicated in the pot culture house attached to the section, in Government Agricultural Stations and in the fields of cultivators under departmental supervision.

*Sugarcane Expert.*—The work of this section is carried out on the Cane Breeding Station, which occupies about fifty-two acres. It is an all-India station started with the object of remedying India's comparatively low outturn per acre of cane. The bulk of India's cane acreage is found in North India and the indigenous canes of that area are in most urgent need of improvement; hence the chief attention of the station is concentrated on work for that area. New types are being raised by growing cane from seed, instead of from cuttings, and crosses are also being made between different varieties.

The original difficulties have been overcome and seedlings are now being raised in large numbers.

Among special subjects being studied are:— The inheritance of characters in seedlings, the nature of the root-system and the fertility of the flower.

Over 300 varieties, collected in India and other countries, are being grown.

*Mycologist.*—Investigation of the fungoid diseases of plants, especially economic crops, and the devising of remedial measures form the main lines of work of this section.

The following are some of the prominent crop diseases that are under investigation at present:—

(1) Green ear disease on cumbu.

(2) Leaf-shredding disease of cholam.

(3) Blast of paddy, ragi and panicum repens.

(4) 'Blights' of paddy.

(5) 'Vermicularia' on chillies, ginger and turmeric.

(6) Smut on sugarcane.

(7) Nut-fall of coconuts.

Methods of control suggested by the Mycologist are being adopted in the case of the following diseases in various parts of the Presidency:—

Bud-rot of palmyras, Mahali or Koleroga of arecanuts, Bleeding disease of coconuts, Mildew on grapevines, Smut on cholam, Scab on lemons.

*Lecturing Systematic Botanist.*—The chief work in this section is teaching. A certain amount of systematic work is, however, carried on in the Herbarium attached to the section.

The collection in the Herbarium represents fully the Phanerogamic flora of the Madras Presidency, and is very valuable, as it contains specimens collected by the famous Botanists, Wight, Beddome, Gamble, Lawson, Bourne, Barber and others. Considerable additions have been made by further collections. This material, placed at Mr. Gamble's disposal for the preparation of the flora of the Madras Presidency, has yielded several species new to science.

A detailed study of the grasses has been undertaken, and the book *A Handbook of South Indian Grasses* was recently published. The weeds growing in cultivated areas are now being studied.

H. C. S.